THE BIG BOOK OF FAMILY FUN

Claudia Arp
and Linda Dillow

A
JANET
THOMA
BOOK

THOMAS NELSON PUBLISHERS

NASHVILLE

The authors and publisher have made every effort to ensure that the activities suggested in this book are safe, as well as fun. However, because of the nature of the materials used, the types of procedures, and the varying ages and skills of your child, we recommend that you supervise your children at all times. The author and publisher cannot be held responsible for injuries that may result from the use of activities recommended in this book.

Published in Nashville, Tennessee, by Janet Thoma Books, a division of Thomas Nelson, Inc., Publishers, and distributed in Canada by Word Communications, Ltd., Richmond, British Columbia, and in the United Kingdom by Word (UK), Ltd., Milton Keynes, England.

ISBN # 0-7852-8200-9

Printed in the United States of America

1 2 3 4 5 6 — 99 98 97 96 95 94

Contents

ACKNOWLEDGMENTS

We are grateful to all the mothers, especially those in PEP Groups for Moms, who shared their fun family adventures with us! Family fun times are like folklore—you may never know the original source. So we wish to thank all who contributed, even those we don't know.

We especially want to thank Suzanne Testerman for all her help in pulling this book together, and Leigh Krieps and Julia Francis Clark, for their creative suggestions for children with special needs.

Special thanks to Susan and Laurie and the in-house staff of Janet Thoma Books and Thomas Nelson Publishers!

To our children and future grandchildren,

Thanks for the fun times you give us.

We've always heard rumors about parents who are naturally creative and full of ideas to keep the family playing and working together. These parents are always smiling, patient, loving, cheerful. Every day they wake up with a song.

We hope you are such a parent, but chances are you're more like we were—often tired and occasionally ready to pull your hair out. Your back pockets hold no ideas for family delights. As we did, you need help: imaginative ideas to build your family unity, communication tips to get your Timmy the Turtle out of his shell, suggestions for building family traditions. So we've pulled together some of the best fun our families ever had, added the fun of members of PEP groups (Parents Encouraging Parents) across America, sprinkled in the fun of some good friends back home, and lovingly wrapped them in this *Big Book of Family Fun* for you and your family.

In this one volume you'll find more than five hundred ways to bring fun into the lives of your children and you: fun for sunny days and indoor days, fun for you and your children with special needs, fun to bring you nearer to those who live far away. The PEP logo next to certain activities indicates that activity as being a contribution of a PEP group member. The Index matches all the activities in the book with the benefits they offer your child. Use this chart as an easy reference. Look for the areas you want your child to develop in and choose the activities that provide growth in those areas.

Some of the suggestions here are "quickies," using materials readily available in every home. Others take planning and preparation. All will build your family unity. And they will be *fun!* This is, after all, the *Big Book of Family Fun!*

CHAPTER 1

Fun in the Sun

*F*rom a safari to the zoo to a wilderness nature hike, outdoor activities can add to your family fun.

Your imagination is your only limit. Here are some suggestions to get your family moving outdoors. Start in your own back yard.

*N*ature Scavenger Hunt

Preparation time is about ten minutes, but the fun for the kids will usually last at least an hour! Make a list of objects for your children to find in your yard or playground. Give them defined boundaries that are safe for their ages.

For small children who do not yet recognize words, use crayons and draw objects for the scavenger hunt. Give each child a list or page with pictures and a bag. Burlap bags with shoulder straps or backpacks work great and make this activity a real hunting adventure. These items are popular with six through eight year olds:

- Rocks (different colors, like a white or a brown one)
- Something fuzzy
- Twig with no leaf
- Twig with a leaf
- Leaves (specified colors)
- Pine cone
- Pine needle
- Dead weed
- Green weed

- Dead bug (for the daring!)
- Moss

After the hunt is over, enjoy a snack and let each child proudly display his treasures. You decide what to do with the dead bug!

*C*olored Chalk Creativity

A big box of colored chalk and a child's great imagination can turn your sidewalk or driveway into a work of art! The kids love drawing on such a large "canvas," and the rain (or hose) will eventually wash it off.

*B*lowing Bubbles!

T his is a fun activity for the whole family; even the adult "kids" enjoy it.

Combine

> 2 c. liquid detergent
> 6 c. water
> 3/4 c. corn syrup

Combine these ingredients in a large bowl or washpan. Dip the large end of a kitchen funnel into the bubble mixture and blow through the small end. You can also make a circle out of a small coat hanger. Dip and blow. The large commercial wands you can buy are fun too.

Nature Hike

Nature hikes can be fun year-round activities. Even in the cold of winter when most foliage is dead, it's possible to find lovely dried leaves and flowers. Talk with your children about what you find:

- How God's colors don't clash
- What kind of leaf you would want to be and why
- What color you would want to be
- How we are all different

Group Fitness

Discuss the importance of conditioning and being in shape. Choose simple exercises and do them together as a family. If you don't know what to do, ask your child's coach for suggestions.

Building Your Own Soccer Goal or Tennis Backboard

A good way to keep your children moving outside is to provide equipment that will help them practice. One dad we know built his sons a soccer goal and provided hours and hours of fun. You can build a tennis backboard out of two-by-fours and treated plywood. Paint it dark green or any color you like.

After the hunt is over, enjoy a snack and let each child proudly display his treasures. You decide what to do with the dead bug!

Garage Sale

Turn your family's trash into other people's treasure by having a garage sale.

You can help your children sort and label items they are ready to give up for the sale. Then, give each of the kids a job for the day of the sale: tending a table or section of the yard, serving refreshments.

Neighborhood Fun

Have the neighborhood kids over for a game of tag, a balloon fight, or a water fight. Better yet, invite the parents too. They can at least watch and sip tea.

Before you know it, you should all be enjoying the sun and surf (water and/or mud). Plan some games like Keep Away or Water Basketball for slack times. You could also play games or cards while waiting for your food to digest before you resume the water fun.

Pool Picnic (or Lake, Beach, River, Mudhole, or Whatever You Can Find)

Let the children plan the picnic menu and, if possible, do the shopping with you. Remember to keep the meal simple: for example, chips, favorite sandwiches, fruit, and juice. Why not let the children make cookies the day before to take on the picnic? (If you're superorganized, you can make the cookies the week before and freeze them for the picnic. However, if time is limited, you can buy cookie doughs that are ready for the oven. Then let the kids decorate them with sprinkles, raisins, and candy.) Now you're ready for your pool picnic!

I've Got a Friend

Y our children can make life livelier for some people who might be lonely or isolated. Make a list of lonely people you know, and call or visit them.

The Elderly

Visit a nursing home or retirement home. You will want to call ahead to find the best time to visit. Ask for the names of people in the home who would welcome visitors. Also ask if you can bring treats or gifts to share. If the answer is yes, the children can make their favorite cookies or brownies to pack in small plastic bags tied with colorful ribbons. You may want to include a verse in each bag, such as Isaiah 46:4:

> *Even to your old age, I am He,*
> *And even to gray hairs I will carry you!*
> *I have made, and I will bear;*
> *Even I will carry, and will deliver.*

Before you go, talk with your children about questions they can ask people, like, "Where were you born?" and "How long have you lived here?" Your kids can also sing a song or read a story.

Church Members

Ask your pastor for the names of lonely people in your church. Bake a treat and take it to one of them. Or send a friendly card to say hello.

Neighbors

Encourage your children to offer to do errands or small chores for someone in your neighborhood who is unable to do errands for himself.

Are you looking for more time for your family? . . . time comes in the little places.

An Outing for Two

Children love going out someplace special, just with you. Consider the following.

School Shopping

Before school starts, plan a back-to-school shopping trip for school supplies, new clothes, or whatever is needed! Have lunch together and talk about the school year ahead.

Walking and Talking

Walking is a lost art but can be lots of fun. Try parking the car several blocks from a special ice-cream shop or restaurant and walk to it to order a big cone for the child (Mom gets a small cone). Then walk back to the car. Of course, if you live near enough, you may not have to use the car at all.

A Bike Hike

Ride bikes on a local biking path or in your neighborhood. Take along a snack. Talk and enjoy the lovely view. Then ride home.

Eating Out

Go wherever your child chooses for lunch. For small children, fast foods are usually the first choice. It gets scary when they're older and begin to choose more expensive places!

Shopping for Others

Together, shop for a gift or a birthday card, and include time for a treat or a short talk.

The Mega Playpen

One mom shared this hilarious story:

"One day I was desperate for some help. My two- and three-year-old boys were full of energy, and I wasn't. The local park I drove to was muddy, and I wasn't in the right frame of mind for the mess. But there was a tennis court there. As I entered the court with my two boys and the tall fence towered over me, I felt as if I received a great revelation from God: 'This is a giant playpen!'

"I closed the gate door behind me. There was no mud. I could sit down on the court and not get wet, and someone had sovereignly left two tennis balls on the courts. The boys had thirty minutes of running, throwing the balls over the net, and working off some of their endless energy while I regained some of mine! Next time I'm taking balls, lunch, blankets, and a book.

A Bus Trip

Find your nearest bus stop and take a short ride. If it's convenient, ride downtown and have lunch or go to a museum. See if you can find any short train trips in your area. This would be fun to do with other families.

An Airport Visit

Visit an airport and watch the planes take off and land.

A Police Station Visit

Call ahead and visit your local police station. Take the officers a treat, such as brownies or cookies, to show your appreciation of their work. You could even make a thank-you poster and have everyone sign it.

A Fire Station Visit

Call ahead and visit a fire station.

Old MacDonald

Visit a working farm so the children can see the animals in their normal environment. If you'll see horses, take carrots or sugar cubes.

Observing the Experts

Take your child to a professional game of her favorite sport. Children learn by watching the experts. If this is not possible in your local area, watch TV sports with your child.

Strawberry Pickin'!

During the spring and summer months, check the classifieds or your local farmers' market for locations of pick-it-yourself places.

Sunday Surprise

Go on a surprise outing every Sunday after lunch. Get on a different bus or train every Sunday and investigate a new area of their city. It is always a surprise because you don't know what you will find. This could be done with a car and a map. Just take off and explore!

CHAPTER 2

Indoor Boredom Busters

*W*hen cabin fever strikes at your house, who you gonna call? Boredom Busters!

From making your own volcano to planting and growing an indoor garden, these indoor games and activities will arm you with enough fun to fill rainy days and snowy days and just plain "I don't have anything to do" days—and to keep them from coming back.

Let's start with something easy.

*T*reasure Hunt

H ide objects throughout your home. Give your child a paper bag and let him have fun hunting for treasures to keep or to eat or to use at play. Favorite objects moms have suggested:

- Pennies
- M&M's
- Healthy snacks like carrot or celery sticks
- Pieces of a super-simple puzzle. (The child can find the pieces and then put the puzzle together.)

*D*ress-up Clothes Box

A box of dress-up clothes (hats, dresses, purses, scarves, belts, sports jackets, and shoes) can keep kids busy for a long time (an old slip makes a great wedding dress). Make sure there is a full-length mirror close by so they can admire themselves and their "finery."

Child's Own Kitchen Drawer

Great for toddlers! Keep a special drawer that is low and easy for your toddlers to open and close. Store plastic containers and tops—anything that doesn't break—and let your toddler play until her heart is content! This is great when you're busy preparing dinner. (A pots-and-pans drawer is also fun. The young child loves the noise, which is fine if you don't have a headache.)

Aggression Cookies

Guaranteed to stomp out grumpiness!

Preheat oven to 350°.

6 c. oatmeal	*3 c. flour*
3 c. brown sugar	*1 t. baking soda*
3 c. margarine	

Mash, knead, and squeeze "until you feel better" and until there are no lumps of margarine. Next, form the dough into small balls, not as big as a walnut, and put on an ungreased cookie sheet. Butter the bottom of a small glass and dip it into granulated sugar; then flatten each ball of dough, dipping the glass into sugar each time.

Bake for 10–12 minutes.

(CAUTION: recipe yields 15 dozen cookies, so you may want to cut the recipe in half unless you want to feed an army!)

Creative Collage

Your cupboard could be the storehouse for the next greatest work of art. You'll need paper—construction paper or computer paper is great—glue, and anything "glueable":

- Egg noodles, spaghetti noodles, macaroni
- Kidney beans, pinto beans, soy beans
- Cheerios, cornflakes, other cereal
- Aluminum foil
- Drinking straws
- Toothpicks
- Raisins, peanuts, marshmallows

The problem with being a parent is that by the time we are qualified, we're also unemployed.

Place all of the "glueable" items in the middle of a table. Then give a piece of paper and a small supply of glue to each of your children (if you can find only one bottle, squeeze a small amount of glue into a paper cupcake holder or onto a piece of foil and let each child use a toothpick to apply the glue).

Your children can then create a masterpiece—perhaps a house with flowers, an animal, or an "original" anything!

After the kids have completed their works of art, have an impromptu art show for family or friends, displaying the masterpieces. (Serve Aggression Cookies.)

A Family Show

Produce your own family video or slide show and have a family night at the movies.

Let the children go through old family slides and/or

pictures—perhaps of them from birth to present, summer vacations, friends, relatives, places you've lived, places you've visited. You can help with the selection (to insure they don't choose any of you in your bathing suit).

If you are preparing a video, have the children draw pictures of family members or special events they remember, or have them dress up as different family members and tell a funny story.

Together, write a script to go with the slides or pictures or acting. Let the children do as much of the creative thinking and writing as possible. Have a "sample" showing when you've completed your work.

Later that evening, or another day, have a showing for the family or perhaps the children's friends. Let the children work the slide projector or VCR and read the script. They will have a good feeling of accomplishment as they create, produce, and direct their own "family movie."

If time permits and you have patience left, make cookies together to serve during the slide show. Good, nutritious, and made without a mixer are Oatmeal Crispies.

*O*atmeal Crispies

■ f you want to, you can cut the sugar in half and substitute about ¼ cup of wheat germ for ¼ cup of the flour. They are more nutritious made this way, though they'll taste better with all the sugar.

Preheat the oven to 350°.

1 c. melted margarine   *3½ c. flour*
1 c. brown sugar   *1 t. salt*

> 1 c. white sugar　　　1 t. soda
> 2 eggs, well beaten　　3 c. quick-cooking oats
> 1 t. vanilla　　　　　　(we have used
> 　　　　　　　　　　　regular oats too)

Mix together melted margarine and sugar; add eggs and vanilla; beat well. Add sifted dry ingredients. Add oatmeal (and nuts if desired). Mix well. Drop by teaspoonfuls onto greased cookie sheets and criss-cross with a fork dipped into flour.

Bake at 350° for ten minutes.

Makes about 5 dozen cookies.

Water Painting

Keep a couple of paint-by-water books in reserve for special times you need a break. Give your child a cup of water, book, and paintbrush. If you don't have a paintbrush handy, Q-tips work great and are less messy than brushes.

A Bowl of Beans

One mom shared, "I always found cooking dinner a chore, because my two-year-old became a leech on my leg, crying, asking me to hold him, asking for juice—you get the picture.

"So I filled a large plastic mixing bowl with dried beans, a wooden spoon for stirring, and plastic cups for scooping and pouring inside the bowl. Then I put a lid on the bowl and stored it on top of the refrigerator.

"When I need some time to complete dinner or another project, I give my son the bowl. I guess for a little boy, playing with those beans is the next best thing to sitting outside and playing in the gravel! And the best thing about this activity is that we can be together while I work."

*R*ainy-Day Chest

Fill a chest or trunk with small, inexpensive games and toys. Wrap each one in Sunday newspaper comics or other colorful paper. Then, on rainy days, open the chest and let each child pick one boredom-buster surprise.

Rainy-day surprises don't have to be expensive. As a matter of fact, it's much better if they are not. Here are some suggestions:

- Inexpensive books
- Liquid bubbles
- Pickup sticks
- Paper dolls
- Puzzles
- Simple craft kits

*F*ood Fun

Gather different food items with varied textures, tastes, and smells. Jell-O, noodles (cooked or dry), grapes, carrots, raisins, vinegar, mayonnaise all work well.

Blindfold your child and have him first touch, then taste (if appropriate) and smell the foods and guess the name of each one. You may want him to wear thin plastic gloves when touching the messier items like mayonnaise.

An Indoor Picnic

Even in inclement weather, you can enjoy a picnic—indoors!

Spread beach towels on the floor and have your child dress in shorts. Serve hot dogs and lemonade. Put dessert treats in sand buckets.

Bagels for Birds

Spread bagels with peanut butter and birdseed. With a string, tie the bagels to a tree near one of your windows. Your children will enjoy watching the birds feast.

You can also learn about the birds of your region if you buy a book of birds. Let the children match the birds that come to eat with the pictures in the book. Then read to the children about those birds.

The Ungame

What kind of animal would you like to be?"

"Describe a happy home."

"What would you like to invent to make life better?"

These are some of the questions asked in a fun game that has helped us to get to know our older children better. It's called the Ungame, and it can be played as a family or alone with one child. This is an excellent boredom buster, or can be used in a Time for Two (see chapter 15 for other Times for Two).

You can buy the Ungame at many Christian bookstores. Also, you can buy separately special cards for parents and teenagers, cards that ask spiritual questions and cards for marriage enrichment (for after the kids are in bed).

*I*ndoor Gardens

Y ou can bring the wonder of gardening indoors with some of the following activities. (After the initial planting, these activities provide fun and times of learning for weeks to come.)

A simple way to do this, and to teach a spiritual lesson at the same time, is to plant together bean seeds, radish seeds, or any fast-growing seeds. Then have your children write one of the following verses on a piece of paper: 1 Peter 2:2; Ephesians 4:15; 2 Peter 3:18; and 1 Thessalonians 3:12.

As you get together to water the seeds each day, you can talk together about how we grow in our Christian lives.

Eggshell Garden

Collect eggshell halves with moist potting soil. Set them in the egg carton. Plant several seeds in each shell.

Use Popsicle sticks to mark the different kinds of seeds. Place in a bright window (southern exposure is best). Keep just barely moist. To transplant outdoors, gently crush eggshells and put the entire plant into the dirt.

Hanging Baskets

You can also start seeds in a hanging basket, or you can transplant the seedlings from the eggshell garden into a hanging basket.

You'll need the following materials:

- Plastic berry basket
- Old pair pantyhose
- Potting soil
- Four pieces yarn, each twelve inches long
- Fast-growing seeds (if you're not transplanting; good seeds to use are those suggested for the eggshell garden and also green beans, lima beans, nasturtiums, marigolds, radishes, carrots)
- Scissors
- Bucket to mix soil

Cut a rectangular piece from the top of the pantyhose. Line the basket. Tie one piece of yarn to the top corners of the basket. Knot the four pieces together at the top so the basket will hang level.

Fill the basket one-half to three-fourths full of moistened potting soil. If you are transplanting, put the roots of the seedlings about ¼″ into the soil. If you are planting seeds, place them just under the surface of the soil. (If you soak the seeds in warm water overnight before planting, they will sprout in three to four days.) Hang the basket outside in a tree once the weather is warm enough. Water when needed.

Sponge Garden

Place a large sponge in a small bowl filled with water. Sprinkle grass seed (or any easy-growing seeds you have) on top of the sponge. Make a chart showing what you do and see each day:

Day 1   Filled with water.
Day 2   Filled again.

See how many days it takes for the seeds to sprout and how fast they grow!

Vegetable Sprouts

Use either a sweet potato or a carrot top for this activity.

If using a sweet potato, insert toothpicks into the potato and place the potato in a jar, resting the toothpicks on the rim of the jar. Add enough water to submerge about one-third of the potato. The pointed end should be down.

If using a carrot, cut about one-half inch off the top. Remove any of the green. Place the carrot in a bowl filled with small pebbles and some water.

Place the jar in the sunlight, and add water as needed. In a few days, a tiny plant will begin to sprout.

Missionary Support

Gain a world view by sending a box of surprises to missionary friends or missionaries your church supports.

Get out a map and identify where the missionaries are living. Try to read a little bit about the area where they live, learning about the culture, the people, the land-scape, and the government.

If you are super-organized, you and the children can write a letter to the family or friends (or call their agency) and ask them what they need. If there is not time for a letter, here are some ideas that are always appreciated:

- Christian books, anything new and stimulating
- Children's books (in many countries it is difficult to find books in English)
- Christian books for children
- Jell-O mixes
- Chocolate chips
- Cake mixes
- Salad dressing mixes
- Spaghetti and sloppy joe mixes
- Games and puzzles for children
- Brown sugar

You can spend an entire indoor day buying, wrapping, and mailing the package. Also, be prepared for the cost of mailing overseas. The cheapest way to mail is the "slow boat" way. It takes a couple of months for packages to get to Europe and much longer to Asia, but what joy your love and thoughtfulness will bring when your special box arrives!

Greeting Card Art

M ake a list of all the birthdays and special occasions for the next few months and spend the day making cards to send to people on the list. You can make get-well cards and cards for Christmas, St. Patrick's Day, Grandparent's

Day, Mother's Day, Father's Day, Easter, as well as for birthdays.

Collect old magazines and old greeting cards, and cut out pictures and verses. Or draw your own pictures and make up your own verses. If you have kept pictures the children have drawn for a slide or video show, or their creative collages, you can use those for greeting cards.

Address envelopes if your cards need them, and write the date the cards are to be mailed in the corner where the stamp goes. Then you can mail the cards on the appropriate day.

Surprises can make tough times easier to bear. Fill someone's closet with balloons. . . . Wear a fake nose to the dinner table.

A Letter a Day

M om's proverb: "In order to receive a letter, one must first write a letter!" So take a day to brush up on everyone's letter writing skills (and catch up on your own correspondence—we have found if parents write letters at the same time as the children, the children are much more willing to keep at it).

While your child chooses someone to write—a friend, grandparent, cousin, aunt, sibling—you can get out stationery. Lined is best for children, but if you don't have any lined stationery, you can make your own with lined paper and stickers.

Teach your child where to write the date and greeting. Discuss what information can go into the letter: What has your child been doing, reading, thinking about? What is he going to do tomorrow and next week? Does she need to say "thank-you" for anything? This might also be a good opportunity to teach dictionary skills for finding words that are hard to spell.

Let younger children write their letters verbally. You can write down exactly what they say and then let them copy. This cuts down on the frustration for the child (and for Mom too) in having to spell every word very, very s-l-o-w-l-y!

If there is time after you have completed your letters, take your child to the post office and let him or her hand the letter directly to the mailperson.

Preparing for the Holidays

G et a jump on upcoming celebrations by making presents or decorations for holidays or birthdays. Pull out the craft supplies and make gifts and decorations for Valentines, Christmas, birthdays, Fourth of July. Don't forget Thanksgiving, President's Day, Martin Luther King, Jr. Day, and St. Patrick's Day.

Gift Art

W ith all of the art your child creates on indoor days, at school, and at Sunday school, he or she will probably produce zillions of artistic masterpieces. But what to do with all of it?

Create a calendar.

Local print/copy stores offer a calendar-making service. You purchase the calendar part, and they will laminate the pictures and bind the calendar.

Call ahead and find out the store nearest you that offers this service. Then have your child choose twelve of his or her favorite pieces and choose which picture will accompany each month.

Go together to the copy shop and have your calendar made.

Tornado in a Jar

The mad scientists in your home will love this activity!

Find an empty jar, one as small as a baby food jar will work. Place a penny in the bottom of the jar, and fill the jar with blue or green dishwashing liquid and water.

Shake and swirl the contents of the jar. Then hold it up and you will see a mini-tornado. It will actually touch down and pull back!

For added excitement, add glitter to your water and watch the show.

Papier-Mâché Volcano

The next time you are shopping for starch, buy the liquid kind and save it for an Indoor Boredom Buster.

Tear a newspaper into strips (your kids will enjoy that!). Then, form your volcano with whatever is in your house that slopes upward and forms a gaping hole, the mouth of the volcano. You could create this by cutting off the tip of a cone-shaped cup. Then dip the newspaper strips into the starch and press the layers onto the cup.

When the volcano dries, find a jar that will fit underneath your volcano. Put about 3 tablespoons of vinegar,

¼ cup of baking soda, and some food coloring into the jar and place it under the volcano.

Watch the volcano erupt with smoke!

Popsicle Stick Art

S ave 'em or buy 'em and put 'em to use (we recommend buying them because the saved ones can be sticky).

The list of things you can create with Popsicle sticks is endless. You can build a house, a fort, or a boat. Or you can pick up a holiday theme and make a reindeer, for example, or a Christmas tree.

Brainstorm ideas with your little ones and have fun.

Coffee Filter Planets

G rab a handful of coffee filters, add some food coloring, and you've got a beautiful planet that needs a name and detailed description and story.

What kind of craft can land on this planet? What is the planet made of? What do the inhabitants (if there are any) eat and drink and wear and sing? How old is this planet?

Your child can write his or her own story about the planet, or tell it to you and let you write it.

Create your own galaxy of questions! (You can also choose a book about planets and the stars to read. Then create a galaxy based on the book.)

*C*reative Drama

Act out a favorite story (maybe the kids will let you play a part) or act out a play from a book of plays you've checked out of the library or bought from your local bookstore. Change the ending of the story, if you like.

As you act, learn theater vocabulary: act, scene, plot, setting, stage right, backstage, finale.

*E*leven Ideas for Learning Something New

Take advantage of your indoor day to teach some basic lessons to your children in fun ways.

1. Buy a chart or open an encyclopedia to help you learn the basic muscles and bones in the body of your child or your child's pets.
2. Learn a new language. Buy language tapes or a children's book in a foreign language. Learn the language together.
3. Learn where all the dishes go so the children can help put away the clean dishes.
4. Discuss basic manners—how to act at a friend's house. To make this fun, compare American traditions to those of another culture; for example, *never* sneeze in public if you are in Austria! If you are in Japan, take off your shoes before you enter a house.

5. Learn the 50 states in America. Then learn the capitals of all the states.

6. Have some water play and learn measurements at the same time. Fill a tub with water and use different size cups and containers to teach what a cup, pint, quart, gallon looks like. You can also take this time to learn the metric system.

7. Learn patterns and sequences using colored blocks, loop cereals, or buttons. Set the objects in order: for example, set up 2 blocks, then 3 blocks; then have your child set up 2 blocks, then 3 blocks. Or you can create a pattern of 1 red block, 2 green blocks, and have your child imitate the pattern.

   If you use buttons or loop cereals, you can string them together after you are through, making a necklace.

8. Have a Left Day or Right Day for your little ones. Wrap different colored bands around their arms. Then throughout the day, ask questions like, "What hand did you use to pick up the paper?" Or, "Would you pass me the peas with your left hand?" Or tell them, "Turn to your left at the end of the hall."

9. Have your child lie down on a huge sheet of paper. Trace her form. Then have her label the major parts of her body: head, arms, hands, feet. Afterward, the two of you can cut the paper into small pieces and make a puzzle.

10. Ask your child to make a map of the house. This will help in learning directional skills.

11. Get an old tube sock and cut off the foot. Put several items which fit into a specific category into a coffee can—like six different things that help you

write. Glue the ankle part of the sock to the top of the can.

Then have your child put her hand into the jar and describe what she feels. This helps her in her ability to express herself and stimulates her sense of touch. As soon as she can, have her name the category for the items.

Nine "Quicky" Boredom Busters

Make a fort throughout a room, using blankets, pillows, cushions, and towels. (If it looks as if you're going to be stuck inside several days, you may want to let the kids leave the fort in place at the end of each day.)

2. With just an ink pad and your fingers, you and your children can make thumb print creatures! Try a mouse or a kitten.

3. Make an "arm tree." Have your child cover his forearm (elbow to wrist) with paint, then press his arm on a piece of paper. This is the "trunk" of the tree.

   He then dips his hand into paint and presses it down at the top of the trunk for the "branches." Using his fingertips, he can make flowers or fruit for the tree. Or he can create a family tree by adding the names of relatives to different "branches."

4. Cut out stencil patterns from clear plastic lids like those on a coffee can and have fun!

5. Using black construction paper and white string, you can create a picture of a skeleton, a dinosaur, a flower, or any number of things.

6. Mix epsom salts and water, and help your child brush the mixture over his or her most recent piece of art. When it dries, he'll have a frosted picture!

7. Create Snoopy characters from lima beans. A lima is the perfect shape for Snoopy's head. Paint the bean white and draw in his features.

   You can also create a Woodstock from a yellow-painted lima and the Great Pumpkin from several orange-painted limas. (You can use these creatures to teach addition and subtraction: Ask, "How many of Snoopy's friends are in the picture?" Then add or take away a character and ask, "Now, how many friends are there?")

8. Give your children long pieces of paper and have them draw their day. They can begin with the sunrise and end with the moon.

9. Bring out the box of sugar cubes or the bag of pretzels for some food art! Gather the kids at the table and let them build a sugar cube igloo or a cabin made of pretzels. Or if you want to avoid "sticky," you can make a tepee of pencils covered with paper.

CHAPTER 3

Whistle While You Work

*I*f your child loves responsibility and likes to work, count yourself among the blessed! Most of us have the other kids, who gripe, sigh, make excuses, and think of ten other things they need to do whenever the dreaded words *work, chores,* or *responsibility* are mentioned. Can work be made fun?

We think it's possible. We also think parents should start as early as possible to teach about the rewards of work—money, personal satisfaction, and maturity. (See page 38 for age-appropriate chores.) Give these activities a try, and see if you hear your children whistling while they work.

*T*he President Is Coming!

M ake helping a game. When you need extra help to tidy up the house quickly, play "The President Is Coming!"

*B*eat the Clock

S et the timer for fifteen minutes and play Beat the Clock. See if the children can complete their jobs before the buzzer rings.

A Zone Offense

D ivide the house into zones, with each family member keeping an area clean. Then have a contest and give rewards for the person with the cleanest zone.

*R*easonable Expectations

*I*n *Mothers & Sons,* Jean Lush (with Pamela Vredevelt) gives the following breakdown of age-appropriate responsibilities:

Ages Two to Four Pick up toys and put away
Clean up dropped food
Choose between two foods at breakfast, make other simple decisions
Simple hygiene—brush teeth, wash and dry hands and face

Ages Four to Five Set the table
Put the groceries away
Feed pets on a schedule
Dust the furniture

Ages Five to Six Help with meal planning and grocery shopping
Make own sandwich or simple breakfast, then clean up
Prepare the dinner table
Make bed and clean room

First Grade Choose clothing for the day
Water plants and flowers
Cook simple foods with help (hot dogs, boiled eggs and toast)
Rake leaves and weeds

Second Grade Oil and care for bike
Take phone messages
Water the lawn
Wash the dog or cat

Third Grade Fold napkins properly and set silverware properly
Straighten closet and drawers
Shop for and select own clothing with parents
Begin to read recipes and cook for the family

Fourth Grade Operate washer and dryer
Prepare a simple family meal
Receive and answer own mail
Wait on guest

Fifth Grade Be alone at home for short periods
Handle sums of money up to five dollars
Maintain personal hobby

Sixth Grade Join outside organizations and do assignments
Put siblings to bed and dress them
Mow lawn with supervision
Schedule time for studies

*B*reakfast Helper

L et the children take turns being the official breakfast helper. The job description for the breakfast helper is to set the table the night before. If it is a cereal morning, your child can put the cereal boxes on the table. It is the breakfast helper's job to get up ten minutes early to be available to help Mom with any last-minute duties.

*F*ifty-two Pick Up

N o, we're not talking about the card game in which you throw down fifty-two cards for some gullible person to pick up. This Fifty-two Pick Up might actually give you a little help!

Set a kitchen timer for fifty-two seconds. See how many items each child can pick up in that time:

- Yesterday's paper
- Umbrella at the back door
- Tennis racket
- Can of tennis balls (counts as three items)
- Wet towels (one point each)
- Dirty socks (one each if even number)
- The last twelve issues of *Reader's Digest*
- Pair of shoes (two points)
- Dirty glasses
- Plate with half-eaten peanut butter sandwich (only one point)
- Half-empty can of soda

The winner is the person who gets closest to picking up fifty-two points.

The Job Jar

Have a job jar. Write each chore on a slip of paper, place the slips in the job jar, and have each person draw for tasks. For difficult tasks, assign job teams.

Do You Live Here?

Before you can expect children to pick up, you must teach them how. A fun game to do this is Do You Live Here?

With your young child, walk up to something in the room and say "Do you live here?" Then pretend that the object you have addressed answers you. For example, you could say to the coffee table, "Coffee table, do you live here?" The coffee table answers, "Yes." Then ask the ball on the floor by the table, "Ball, do you live here?" Let your child answer for the ball, "No, I don't live here. I live in the toy box." Then let the child take the ball to its home, the toy box. Continue the game as long as your child will participate and it's fun.

Alphabet Pick-Up

A variation of Do You Live Here? is to use sounds or letters of the alphabet. "Can you find something that needs to be picked up that begins with a *B* sound?" Your child might find the book on the couch that needs to be returned to the bookshelf. Another optional pick-up activity is to let your child find two things on the floor that don't belong there or two things on the table that need to be put away.

*C*harting It Out

C harts can let children know what is expected of them and help parents to follow through. The secret of using charts effectively is changing and switching them. Consider weekly charts, one-time charts, or perhaps even a morning checklist like the following.

> Before I leave for school this morning I will
> ____ Get up on time on my own
> ____ Get dressed
> ____ Make my bed
> ____ Eat breakfast
> ____ Brush my teeth
> ____ Comb my hair

Another idea is to use a chart for a certain period of time with a starting and an ending date, for example, Saturday through Friday. We've included a sample weekly chart on page 42.

If you want to reward your child's work with an allowance, you can establish an amount you'll pay for each task—say, five cents. Then, at the end of the week, you can add the chores completed and pay the specified sum.

How much time does it take to talk to a five year old? As much as you can find. But you're certain to find more of it if you make the most of life's many small situations!

Jobs for Jodie

	Sat.	Sun.	Mon.	Tue.	Wed.	Thu.	Fri.
Make bed	✓	✓					✓
Clean room	✓	✓					
Clean hamster cage—Mon							
Special job							
Clean my dresser							✓
Brush teeth twice—daily							
Pick up cat toys—Mon.							
Feed cat 4 times— Sun., Tue., Thu., Sat.							
Clean my part of bookshelf							
Lay out clothes and school pack before going to bed							
Brush cat—Wed., Fri.							
Dust my part of room—Sun							

Or you may prefer to establish a weekly allowance the child can count on, and pay an additional sum for each chore completed. With either system, a weekly chart can help you and your child keep track of the chores completed.

*B*rainstorming

Why not have a brainstorming session with your children and list together ideas for summer jobs. Below are some of the ideas that came up in one family that did this:

- Have a yard sale
- Grow tomatoes and cucumbers and sell to neighbors (They said to forget zucchini because everyone has plenty.)
- Do yard work (mow, pull weeds, plant flowers)
- Water yards and plants on a regular basis for neighbors
- Teach younger children a sport—soccer, tennis, basketball
- Provide the entertainment for birthday parties
- Deliver balloons for special occasions
- Babysit

The list can go on and on. Consider these fun ways for your kids to earn money:

- Pet sitting
- Dog walking
- Reading to senior citizens
- Assisting at parties
- Emptying trash
- Cleaning and organizing attics and garages
- Cleaning out crawl spaces and storage sheds
- Simple home maintenance projects
- House sitting
- Gofering
- Typing and word processing
- Letter writing for elderly people
- Selling toys (children's version of a garage sale)
- Making and selling Christmas tree decorations
- Making and selling Christmas wreaths
- Delivering papers
- Any other ideas you and your family think up

*H*ow the Ants Do It

A s you teach your children good attitudes and diligence, consider ants. Have you ever watched ants carry tiny bits of food? Where do the ants take the food? What do they eat in the winter when it's cold and they can't find food?

Read Proverbs 30:25 in the Living Bible. Use felt pens to make posters of ants. Write the Bible verse on it, or make your own paraphrase: "Remember the ants—save a dime for later."

To see some ants actually at work, you may want to purchase an ant farm from your hobby store; or track a busy neighborhood colony.

*G*ive, Earn, Save, Spend Game

W rite the words *Give, Earn, Save,* and *Spend* on separate index cards for each family member.

Take turns making up situations that could involve giving, earning, saving, or spending. Then read one statement at a time to the rest of the family.

After a statement is read, have each person hold up a card that declares his initial reaction to the situation. Discuss your responses. What are the advantages of giving, earning, saving, or spending in each situation?

Examples of statements you might use are:

- "Your grandparents gave you a gift of ten dollars for Christmas."

- "Your best friend's birthday is next week."
- "Your church is putting together food baskets for needy families for Thanksgiving."
- "The ball game is next Friday night."
- "You received five requests for donation in the mail today."
- "You earned ten dollars cleaning out the garage."

*E*asy-to-Make Banks

Cut a slit in the lid of a margarine tub. Let your child decorate the tub with stickers, self-adhesive vinyl, or permanent-ink felt pens. Your child can drop her savings into this bank she made.

A Skills Clinic

Check with your church sports ministry or youth director or with a school or league coach and find kids who have the skills your child needs to develop and who want to earn some money while helping younger children.

Set a time and place, like every Monday afternoon right after school in your yard. Call the parents of your child's friends who are also involved in the same sport (or would like to be). Invite their children to participate. Each child pays a fee for each clinic—like two dollars per afternoon.

Provide snacks and drinks for the hungry mob.

Then watch as your child builds confidence and enjoyment in this sports activity.

Challenge your child to keep his room neat for twenty-one days straight. If he misses a day, he has to start counting days all over again.

Seventy-five Cents a Book

Want to encourage your child in reading, neatness, and spelling? Here's an idea.

Incorporate into the children's goals some activities that will give them an advantage when school starts again. Ben was an okay student, but neatness and spelling were definitely not his strong suits. So his parents designed a reading program to help him improve these skills. He likes to read, so they selected a group of books from which he could choose. For each book that Ben read, wrote a report on (neatly), and learned to spell the misspelled words, he earned seventy-five cents. If he finished ten books, he would get an extra five dollars.

He didn't finish all ten books—actually it was several less. But even though he didn't reach his original goal, Ben felt good about himself, for he accomplished more than if his family had not taken the time to set a goal. And when the new school year started, his neatness and spelling improved. And he was more interested in reading.

Freebies

When your children run out of people to write, send away for free information. This is a constructive and fun project, and they will love getting mail back—especially if they are patient. It usually takes four to six weeks for a reply.

For an up-to-date list of "freebies," we suggest the book *Free Stuff for Kids* published yearly by Meadowbrook.

Check your local bookstore or library for other freebie books.

Watch magazines and the backs of cereal boxes for other free offers.

CHAPTER 4

Crafty Kids

*C*rafty kids are clever kids—they learn to see the world and its materials with inventive eyes. Clear the table, get out the glue, and have fun!

Let's Crochet

Y our child can crochet (or loop by hand) a chain-stitch picture to adorn the kitchen wall, his or her bedroom, Grandmother's bedroom wall.

Pass hook under yarn and catch yarn with hook (see #1 of the diagram in the right margin). This is called yarn over hook.

Draw yarn through loop on hook (step #2). Do not work tightly. One chain stitch is completed.

Continue to yarn over and draw through a new loop (step #3) for the number of chain stitches required. Keep thumb and forefinger near the stitch you are working on. This keeps the chain from twisting.

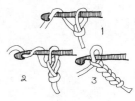

Try "yarn looping"—it's even simpler. Make a slipknot at one end of the yarn (step #1).

Make a loop to the left of the slipknot. Put the new loop through the original loop and pull snugly on the new loop (step #2).

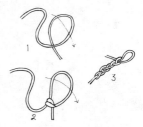

Continue in this manner, keeping the working loop on the right large enough to put the new loop through. When the yarn is used up (or is long enough), put the end through the last loop and pull tight. This is like crocheting but without the hook.

Creative Clay

This activity is quite versatile. Children of all ages enjoy the sensation of working with modeling clay, and the end product is limited only by age, time, and creativity. Here are three economical recipes you can make at home.

Creative Clay

> 1 c. cornstarch
> 2 c. baking soda (1-lb. package)
> 1¼ c. cold water

Stir starch and soda together. Mix in cold water and stir over heat until mixture has consistency of mashed potatoes. Turn onto a plate and cover with a damp cloth until cool enough to handle.

Then knead. Use immediately or store in an airtight container. This dough has a smooth consistency. It is good for ornaments, modeling, or pottery. It can be rolled thin and cut with cookie cutters. Dry it at room temperature for three days, or put it in a 200° oven until it's dry.

Favorite Play Dough

> 2 c. flour   2 c. water
> 1 c. salt   2 T salad oil
> 4 t. cream of tartar   food coloring

Cook over medium heat until a soft, lumpy ball forms. It happens quickly. Knead for a few minutes until dough is smooth. Store in an airtight container. Dough can be frozen and refrozen several times.

Why not use Christmas cookie cutters with your dough and make Christmas tree decorations for your family and for Christmas gifts?

Another suggestion is to make little figures (like Fisher Price people) for the nativity scene—they can be quite rustic. Let them dry and then paint them (use tempera paints). Pack them away safely. Then before Christmas take a walk through the woods and pick up moss, roots, acorns, sticks, stones—anything of interest. Bring them home and, on a piece of plywood, construct your own nativity scene. Collect extra items for grandparents and build another one for them.

Do the same for other holidays or do a set of figurines that look like your family. Update them every few years.

Kool-Aid Play Dough

Mix well

2½ c. flour	1 T alum
½ c. salt	2 pkgs. unsweetened Kool-Aid

Add

2 c. boiling water
3 t. cooking oil

Knead until smooth. Let the play dough cool.

Play Dough Tips

A coffee can lined with a plastic bag makes a good storage container for dough.

If you choose a recipe with no oil in it, it will dry hard and you can paint it with tempera.

If you leave the food coloring out while you're mixing, it can be added as you play.

Adding a flavor extract like lemon or vanilla will make the dough smell good.

Use waxed paper on the table as you play.

Varnish or shellac a finished product to preserve it.

Know you what it is to be a child? It is . . . to believe in love, to believe in loveliness.

Francis Thompson
*Shelley, In
Dublin Review*

*F*inger Painting

A nother good indoor activity is finger painting. Here are three different ways to make the paint.

Finger Paints

> *1 c. soap flakes*
> *dry tempera or food coloring*
> *1/2 c. water*

Whip flakes and water until thick and smooth. Stir in color, if desired. Use a blob on slick-finished paper.

Pudding Finger Paints

To make this type of finger paints for the kids who get more paint in their mouths than on the paper, put dabs of pudding at each child's place on a vinyl tablecloth. Let them have a delicious time!

Would You Believe Shaving Cream?

Squirt a bit of aerosol shaving cream on paper. Add a few drops of tempera paint and you have instant finger paint.

*F*abric Yarn Cards

M ake a card and send it to an elderly relative or hospital patient (you can ask your pastor for names). Perhaps you could use Indoor Day or a Time for Two to make several fabric yarn cards to send to lonely people.

You'll need to gather

- Fabric scraps
- Yarn scraps
- Scissors
- Glue
- Construction paper

First cut the construction paper into a size that will fit in an envelope (or make a big card and mail it in a manila envelope). If desired, your child can first draw a design or picture on the card with a pencil, then cut out fabric and yarn and paste it on the outline to make a beautiful fabric and yarn collage picture card.

*F*ingerprint Cards

W hy not make Fingerprint Cards to send to Grandmother or other relatives or friends? Gather

- Sheets of white paper or construction paper cut to make a card
- Scissors
- Ink pad
- Color markers or crayons

After you have cut the paper in the shape you want the card to be, have children press their fingers one at a time on the ink pad and then on their cards. Flowers, bees, mice, and any number of designs and pictures can be created. The markers or crayons can be used to add stems to the flowers or wings to the bees.

Picture Story

Cut out pictures from magazines. Tape them to a spiral notebook or other blank book. Have your child make up a story using the pictures as illustrations.

Sponge Chart

Cut number shapes out of sponges and use tempera paint to make a collage. Using the same sponges, make a measuring chart for your child on the inside of a closet, using a cheery sticker to mark her current height. Include the date.

Bookmark

Make a bookmark using ribbon and felt; cardboard and wrapping paper; cross-stitch material and floss.

Or cut construction paper into strips 6″ long by 2″ wide. Punch a hole through one end, and thread a ribbon through it. Glue on pictures, stick on stickers, or create designs with crayons or markers.

*F*all Centerpiece

In the fall gather leaves, acorns, pine cones, and such, and design a centerpiece for the table.

*S*hoebox Fun!

Make a bus, train, airplane, or boat from a shoebox. Tie several together with string to make a train. Decorate inside and out with stickers and markers.

*F*all Wax Designs

Collect some beautiful leaves from your yard and make a fancy collage. Place the leaves on a sheet of wax paper. Remove the paper from a few crayons and scrape shavings from the crayons onto the leaves and paper. Sprinkle some glitter over everything, and then cover with another sheet of wax paper. Mom can then help the child iron over the wax paper using a medium-hot iron until all the wax melts into the leaves. The design will be permanent and perfect for a window, refrigerator, or bulletin board.

*R*ubbings

Taking simple household objects, putting a piece of paper over them, and rubbing them lightly with a crayon or pencil sounds too easy to be fun. But try it. Use this technique with things like coins, necklaces, or paper clips—anything fairly flat. The shape will appear on your paper.

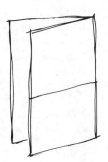

*R*ain Gauge

You will need a six-inch ruler, some transparent tape, and a drinking glass or jar with straight sides. Fasten the ruler onto the side of the jar with tape. Set the glass outside when it looks like it will rain, being sure to place it away from buildings or trees. Compare your results with those on the TV weather report.

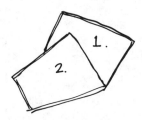

*M*aking a Snowflake

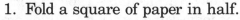

Follow these steps for creating a snowflake. Use the illustrations to help.

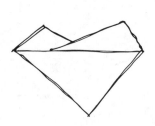

1. Fold a square of paper in half.
2. Mark the center of the folded square as shown.
3. Fold it again like this. Mark the parts 1 and 2.
4. Fold 1 over 2 and then turn the paper over.
5. Draw a design up to the arrow and cut it out without unfolding.

6. The cut-out design is your paper snowflake. Draw different designs, and you will have a collection of paper snowflakes.

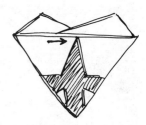

*T*oothpick Sculptures

ou will need toothpicks and marshmallows.

Use the marshmallows to hold the toothpicks together as you build a sculpture.

*H*ole Punching

ne fun activity with paper is hole punching. Let your child punch holes in colored paper. The confetti that falls to the floor or on the table makes great fine motor pincer play for the younger child. Eventually children can collect it and glue it onto paper or use it to decorate the outsides of small plastic containers. When your child gets tired of confetti play, the mess is easy to vacuum up.

*M*ixing Colors

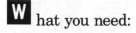hat you need:

- Four glasses
- Water
- Yellow, red, and blue food coloring

Fill three glasses with water and have your child put drops of each color into separate glasses to make blue, yellow, and red water. Now your child can mix the colored water in the other glass to see what colors they can make.

Yellow and red will make orange; yellow and blue will make green; and blue and red will make violet.

Mobiles

M aterials:

- Wire coat hanger
- String
- Cardboard or construction paper
- Aluminum foil
- Paints and brushes
- Crayons

Cut pieces of string of random lengths, and tie them to the bottom of a wire coat hanger. Cut different shapes— hearts, birds, animals, and so on—from construction paper or foil. Decorate with paints or crayons.

Tie each shape to a piece of string and hang from your wire mobile. Suspend your mobile from a single string in a spot where air currents will keep the hanger and decorations moving.

People Printing

O n a sunny day, let your child paint her hands and feet with easel paint; then quickly place them on a large piece of blank paper. You can frame it, or they can just be silly and hop around.

Who Needs a Brush to Paint?

If you're willing to brave a mess, let your child paint without brushes—use something else! Try Q-Tips, an old toothbrush, an eye dropper, an old bottle brush, an old roll-on deodorant bottle filled with paint, sponges, cookie cutters, bottle caps, crumpled paper, pine needles, or the skins of oranges.

Go Fishing

Dental floss fastened to a straw with a paperclip hook makes a rod. A small pan of water or a baby pool becomes the river. Fish or bathtub creatures cut from foam sponges add to the adventure.

Air Tanks

Tape together two empty 2-liter soft drink bottles with electrical tape or masking tape. Loops made from tape can fashion these air tanks into a young scuba diver's or astronaut's back.

*B*inoculars

Tape two empty toilet paper rolls side by side; then fasten a yarn loop to them. These make-believe binoculars help a child become an outdoor adventurer. Add a magnifying glass to gain a different perspective on grass, leaves, and the entire outdoors.

*D*ig This Fun!

Most children like to dig in the dirt, so instead of frowning on this dirty activity, define a small area with railroad ties or an old tire. Inside that digging spot, children can happily shovel away.

*F*luffy Friends

Choose a piece of construction paper that would make a good sky. Think about the shapes you have seen the clouds make in the sky or what shapes you would like to see. Draw an outline of your favorite cloud shapes, or just begin by pasting down pieces of cotton and pushing them around until you get the shapes you like best.

*P*uzzles by You

Make your own puzzles! Get a thin piece of cardboard and a favorite picture. Trim them to the same size. Paste the picture onto the cardboard. Now turn the cardboard over so you can't see the picture. Draw the shapes of puzzle pieces onto the cardboard, and then cut carefully along those lines. Turn the pieces right side up and put them together again.

*M*arble Art

F or this work of art you need

- Marbles
- A clear plastic lid
- Many paint colors

Put your colors in various places on the lid; add marbles; swirl and gently tilt the lid as the marbles roll through the paint. These turn out to be beautiful!

*P*asta Colors

I f you are planning to string macaroni or use noodles in a collage, try this first! In a baggie, add alcohol to a favorite shade of food coloring. Put in your macaroni and leave it overnight. In the morning the noodles will be that color.

If I could go through it all again, the slender iron rungs of growing up, I would be as young as any, a child lost in unreality and loud music.

Robert Traill
Spence Lowell
Realities

CHAPTER 5

Creative Recycling

*B*efore you throw it away, think about it! Children are never too young to learn to recycle. They can discover how to use and adapt what they already possess. Paper bags, egg cartons, boxes, old magazines, and colored eggshells creatively become mosaics, houses, and butterflies. These activities are fun and they teach our children to respect, love, and take care of God's world.

*T*hings to Save/Things to Make

Save	*Make*
• Paper rolls	Telescope, megaphone, binoculars
• Oatmeal boxes	Rocket ships, drums
• Milk cartons	Pull trains and blocks
• Shoeboxes	Doll house rooms
• Sheets	Tent, sleeping bags
• Empty cans, string	Telephone, stilts
• Egg and milk cartons	Castle, caterpillar
• Socks, nylons	Sock puppets, old faces
• Corks, sponges	Boats
• Boxes of all sizes	Cage, doll bed and house, cars, planes, trucks, barn
• Paperclips	Necklace, other jewelry

*G*arbage Gobbler

W ash and dry a large bleach bottle. Cut the top almost all the way off, leaving a hinge near the handle. Cut out

and glue paper face features and yarn hair onto the bottle. Then keep the room clean by feeding all your garbage to the Gobbler!

*M*ilk Carton Birdfeeder

M ake a birdfeeder by cutting one side from a half-gallon milk carton, leaving the edge on the bottom. Make a hole through the bottom side of the carton and insert a small branch from a tree. Place a heavy rock in the bottom, and fill with bird seed!

*O*atmeal Drum

R ecycle your oatmeal box by making a drum! Paint or contact paper the box with a dark color. Cut out two circles of felt, making sure they are larger than the top of the box. Punch an equal number of holes in each circle with a hole puncher or a sharp pencil. Place one circle on top of the box, one on the bottom. Thread them together with a long piece of yarn. Glue feathers to the side of the box and *voilà!* An official drum.

*P*aper Bag Faces

M aterials:

- Paper bags
- Cotton puffs
- Yarn
- Crayons
- Scissors
- Glue

Depending on the size of the bag used, these can be either hand puppets or actual children's masks. Cut holes for eyes, nose, and mouth. Use the yarn to decorate the head with hair, mustaches, or beards. Glue on cotton puffs for eyebrows or cheeks. Color with felt-tip pens or crayons.

For a fun variation, use paper plates to make the faces, and tie the plates on the children with yarn or ribbon. Make headbands out of construction paper and decorate them with glitter or color designs. Tie them on with string.

*C*rawling Alligator

C ut wedges from a tissue box.

Cover the shapes with green paper. Glue the larger ends of the wedges together.

To make the eyes, glue cotton balls on the shorter wedge; use dark paper for the pupils. Glue paper for the mouth and nose, or draw them on with marker or crayon.

Thread a straw or a pipe cleaner through a spool of thread for a wheel and axle. Poke holes in the larger wedges to place the axle on the inside.

A Box Fort

S ave large boxes for your child to make her own fort, house, or slide. One mom shared how her daughter created a house, drew in windows with curtains and a mailbox, and used magazine pictures to decorate with flowers.

*H*ome Decorating

On a large piece of paper (like butcher paper), draw a house frame showing the different rooms, and tape it to a door or a wall. Give your children old catalogs, and let them cut or tear out pictures of furniture, lamps, pictures, people, or anything they want to place in the rooms. Let them paste or tape objects within the house—not on your walls.

*P*aper Collage

Using old magazines and catalogs, let your child make a collage of things in God's world that are good for you or things he is thankful for. This will help develop cutting, tearing, and pasting skills and will keep your child busy for quite a while.

One mom shared recently that her two children did this activity together on paper plates and got along great, which was quite unusual for them.

*B*asket Sledding

Next snow, go sledding! Tie a rope to an old laundry basket and pull your children around.

*P*aper Magic

See how many different kinds of paper your children can find in your home. Almost any kind of paper can be used to create your own magic. Look for

- Construction paper
- Typing paper
- Newsprint
- Cardboard
- Crêpe paper
- Tissue paper
- Wallpaper samples
- Newspapers
- Catalogs
- Magazines
- Grocery bags
- Gift wrapping
- Wax paper
- Paper towels
- Facial tissues
- Paper napkins

Cut the paper into various shapes—dolls, dogs, stars, snowflakes. Or tear the paper into tiny pieces. Draw a picture on a plain sheet of white or colored construction paper. Trace the outline of the drawing or fill it in with glue. Then sprinkle the tiny pieces of paper over the drawing. Shake off the excess paper. Now you have a mosaic!

A child said
What is grass?
fetching it to me
with full hands.

Walt Whitman
Song of Myself

*L*iving Paper

Paper can do many things. It starts out flat, and you can put life into it by

- Cutting
- Tearing
- Bending
- Curling
- Scoring
- Twisting
- Wrinkling
- Punching
- Interlacing
- Pasting

- Fringing
- Scratching
- Folding
- Denting
- Pinching

- Stapling
- Stapling
- Marking
- Painting
- Papier mâchéing

*E*gg Carton Caterpillar

Materials:

- Empty egg carton
- Pipe cleaners
- Paint and/or crayons
- Construction paper
- Scissors
- Glue

Carefully cut the carton in half lengthwise so that the caterpillar has six connected humps when it's turned over. Puncture each hump and insert a pipe cleaner through each segment to form the legs. Cut out paper eyes, nose, and mouth, and glue them to the front section of the egg carton. Color the segments with crayons or paint.

*E*ggshell Butterflies

Using leftover colored eggshells from your children's Easter baskets, yarn or magic markers, and heavyweight paper, make a butterfly or any other "critter" your children's imaginations can conceive. Outline a butterfly with magic marker or yarn on the heavy paper. Glue the colorful eggshells inside the butterfly's wings, creating a multicolored collage. If a pastel butterfly is desired, use pink, yellow, and powder blue shells.

If butterflies aren't your "thing," create a stained-glass window with your eggshells.

*B*ecome an Ecology Expert

W ith kids' ecology becoming very popular, this is a good time to encourage your children to write off for kids' information kits about the environment. Ask your child to specify whether she wants the kit for grades K–6 or for grades 7–12. Your children can address their requests to

> Environmental Protection Agency
> Public Info Center
> PM 211B
> 41 M Street, SW
> Washington, D.C. 20460

CHAPTER 6

School Days

*H*omework hassles may be history with the following school-day sanity savers! From homework helper boxes to breakfast quickies and prepackaged clothes, we promise you your school days can be more fun.

A Homework Center

Most parents provide a desk or place to study in their children's rooms. Yet most children study somewhere else! Why? If your kids are like most kids, they want to be near the hub of activity, and their rooms just don't qualify.

One mom found a great solution. She created a homework center right around the kitchen table. A file box held school supplies that were readily available and also could be put away quickly when her homework center became the evening dinner table. She also took time each afternoon to be on call at the homework center to answer questions and encourage her two children.

*P*repackaged School Clothes

The next time you do laundry, recruit your child to help. As you are folding the clothes, let your child put several school outfits together—complete with socks, underwear, ribbons, belts, jeans, and whatever else makes up a complete outfit. Then package each outfit or hand the outfits together on coat hangers, and place them in your child's closet. On busy mornings, instead of calling, "Mom, what can I wear?" your child can make a personal selection in record time.

And just think—it may match!

A Homework Helper Box

Purchase a cardboard storage box. Let your children decorate the outside of the box with stickers and stencils. Put needed school supplies in the box. You might include

- Paper
- Pencil sharpener
- Felt-tip pens
- Scissors
- Dictionary
- Markers

- Pencils
- Glue sticks
- Rulers
- Theme folders
- Thesaurus

A Trip to an Office Supply Store

I don't know what it is about families, but most of us love office supply stores. So don't miss out on a fun field trip with your child. Go to an office supply store, and purchase your supplies for your Homework Helper Box. You can even get the box there! Remember to make a list of what you need *before* you go to the store.

*R*ecord-a-Homework

To keep an accurate record of homework assignments and accomplishments, record both. Use a portable cassette recorder, and let each child have a tape and make daily recordings. For double entry, write assignments and completions in a homework notebook as well.

A Morning Devotion Time

Make family devotions a natural part of your morning routine. We found that if we read just one Bible verse and prayed together, our days went much, much better.

Keep it simple. We had our devotion time as part of our breakfast. It rarely lasted over five minutes. This made it practical enough that we actually did it!

Keep it relevant. If a child has a test that day, he'll be willing to have you join him in praying for him to do his best.

Use simple helps, and change them from time to time. We used successfully a devotional guide to Scripture reading, *The Living Light* (Tyndale, Wheaton, IL), and *A Bread Loaf of Bible Verses* (Warner Press, Anderson, IN). Each day you choose one verse from the small "loaf" of bread, read the verse, and discuss it. We have also used calendars with a verse a day. Or you could make your own jar of Bible verses. Let each child write out several favorite verses, fold each verse separately, and put the slips in a jar. Take turns drawing a verse to read at breakfast.

Here are two ideas for helping your child start the day with a good attitude and a full stomach.

Tips for parent-teacher conferences:

1. Prepare for the meeting ahead of time.

2. Be willing to ask questions.

3. Explain any special experiences or schooling your child has had.

4. Let the teacher know you want to help.

*B*randed Pancakes

Make pancakes as directed on Bisquick package. Let batter trickle from teaspoon onto hot griddle to form a letter. Letters must be made backward to be right when the pancakes are served. Draw your initial backward on a piece of paper before you start.

When the bottom side of the initial has lightly browned, pour a regular spoonful of pancake batter over the initial.

Bake until bubbles appear, then turn and finish cooking.

Serve these personalized pancakes hot with butter and warm syrup or jelly.

*B*reakfast Quickies

Toast Toppers

Dress toast up with these toast toppers:

- *Orange Sugar*—Blend 1 T soft butter and 3 T sifted powdered sugar. Stir in 1 t. grated orange rind and 1 t. orange juice. Spread on unbuttered toast.
- *Cinnamon Mix*—Combine 1 t. cinnamon and 2 T sugar. Sprinkle on hot buttered toast. Cut the toast in strips.
- *Raisin Peanut Butter*—Mix ½ c. crunchy peanut butter, 2 T chopped seedless raisins, and 2 T orange juice. Spread on hot toast.

Breakfast Fruit Treats

- *Taste of Hawaii*—strawberries and pineapple chunks
- *Tropical Morning*—sliced bananas in orange juice
- *Polka-Dot Day Brightener*—raisins sprinkled on apple-sauce
- *Cool Combo*—strawberries and seedless grapes

Tricks and Treats with Cereals

- Strawberries over a big bowl of Wheaties
- A raisin face in a bowl of instant oatmeal or Cream of Wheat
- A bowl of Cheerios topped with half a peach with raisin eyes, a cherry nose, and an apple slice mouth

First Day of Winter Time for Two

T o let your child know you understand, plan a special time for the first day of winter. You may even be starting a new winter tradition! Be ready to listen to all the details of what is going on at school.

On the first day of winter (or spring) arrange to pick up your child after school and stop off for a cup of hot chocolate or your child's favorite snack. If your child is normally quiet, have your own list of questions ready. Or use some of these open-ended statements:

- What I like most about school this year is . . .
- What I like least about school this year is . . .
- My favorite class . . .
- My least favorite class . . .

- My best friend . . .
- My favorite school lunch . . .
- My most difficult assignment . . .
- My goal for the year is . . .

School Lunch Date

You may want to give your child a written invitation. You could even send it through the mail. Show me a child, and we'll show you someone who enjoys getting personal mail.

This activity is great for younger children. But be forewarned: If your child is in middle school or high school, please check first. Chances are she would rather not eat than be caught in the school cafeteria with Mom or Dad.

Positive Lunch Notes

Keep cards, stickers, and felt-tip pen handy. You might keep them in a drawer in the kitchen. Tom got a sticker and a short note on his napkin in his lunch box each school day. It was simple for his mom to remind him how special he was!

The At-Least-Fifteen-Minutes- a-Day Tradition

How can you teach a child to study if the child says every day, "I don't have any homework"? Start the fifteen-minutes-a-day study tradition. If your child has no homework, provide a fifteen-minute reading assignment or activity to help her develop the habit of studying and to broaden her knowledge. For an occasional treat, provide her with an educational video to watch.

*L*et's Type

N ot every mother would let her children do this," says one mother, "but I have an older typewriter, and I let my child type. Since he's just learned his alphabet, he loves this. All I have to do is put the paper in the typewriter."

Try this with your home computer if you dare! Even studying for a spelling test can be fun when your child types in the words—correctly spelled—and chooses a font or style for printing them out.

A Mom's School for Younger Children

A younger child who doesn't have any homework may feel left out. Look at the child's papers, and give some homework. You could assign a page to color or writing a page of ABCs or numbers. Reward the effort with a sticker treat.

For the child who complains about bedtime being too early, let him have extra time if he reads in bed.

A Positive Sandwich

S ometimes your child comes home with negative feelings. It's okay to express negative feelings, but help the child do it in a positive way, maybe with a "positive sandwich." The idea is to cushion the negative statement between two positive statements. For example, your child might say, "I had a great time playing on the playground today, but Joey called me a nerd. The good news is my friends said I was nice, not nerdy!"

Dad could say, "I really appreciate your attempt to clean your room, but clothes under the bed are unacceptable! On the other hand, your desk is well organized. Now what can you do about the clothes?"

Let early
education
be a sort of
amusement;
you will then
be better able
to find out the
natural bent.

Plato
The Republic, VII

*G*ood and Bad Days

E veryone has them! Give your child a way to vent frustration or jubilation by giving your child a journal. On especially bad days, have your child write down what makes him mad. On good days, have him write down what made him glad! Not only is this therapeutic, but it also provides a good laugh once your child has grown.

If your child has a bad day at school or gets a bad grade, you can help to restore his confidence. Sit and listen to him; he needs your time and your full attention. Do something physical with the child—basketball, Ping Pong, or rollerblading. Have an Honor Night, like a special person party. Write a note or a poem and tape it to his toothbrush or pin it to his pillow case. If you read

Philippians 4:8 together and make a list together of the positive things you can think about, you will help your child begin to think on the positive even in a bad situation.

CHAPTER 7

Family Togetherness

*T*he sun sets and everyone bounds home, energy and restlessness in tow! Here are more than twenty-five activities for the entire troop to enjoy.

Family Nights are planned times when you are alone together as a family. It is a time to relax and enjoy being together. While Family Night may be an excellent time to work on instilling values and teaching spiritual truths, it is also a time to have fun. Often values will be caught, not taught. Over the years, a high priority for us was simply to have fun together. Here are some guidelines for Family Night:

- Don't overstructure your Family Night. Much of the year our children are in school five days a week, and their time at school is very structured. They won't get excited about Family Night if it feels like school.
- Be flexible. You may have chosen your favorite game to play when everyone else is in the mood to read the book you just bought. Relax and trust the group. Go with the flow!
- Consider your objectives—to build strong relationships and strengthen your own family unit and just to have fun!
- Know your family and plan appropriately.
- Relax. Everything doesn't always have to work out perfectly. Just clean up the messes and move on!

*D*innertime Shuffle

L et everyone sit in someone else's place at the dinner table and act like that person. Be prepared for an interesting meal! One psychologist who actually did this in his family said he could have written some new case studies with his family as the subjects. He saw himself in a completely different light through the eyes, conversation, and actions of his ten-year-old daughter, who sat in his place at the dinner table!

Family Concert Hall

A child who plays an instrument can organize a concert for the family (and later for neighbors, friends, etc.). The child can make programs about the presentation. A sibling or parent can help by baking cookies for the family spectators. Be sure to tape—better yet, videotape—the performance and send it to grandparents and others who live far away. This is a stimulating way to honor a child's accomplishment and have fun as a family!

Table Fables

After dinner, while everyone is still at the table, have everyone choose an animal he or she would like to be. Taking turns, each "animal" can pretend he is on a journey from the beach to the forest, or through the jungles, and tell the other family members about the adventure.

The Listening Game I

First, ask your children questions designed to give you more insight into them as people. Then concentrate on really listening to their responses. Try some of these open-ended statements:

- If I had three wishes, I'd wish for . . . *easy bake*
- My favorite food is . . . *broccilli,*
- My favorite color is ___*yellow*___ because . . . *it is the color of the sun.*
- My pet peeve is . . . *Heather bugs mean the*
- My favorite book is . . . *This one*
- The thing I like most about my family is . . . *we go places*
- When I grow up, I'd like to be . . . *a rock star.*
- My best friend is . . . *Linda*
- Sometimes I feel . . . *happy*
- If I were a parent, I would . . . *make rules*
- I worry about . . .
- What I like best about myself is . . .

*T*he Listening Game II

T his version of the Listening Game is more suitable for older children and teenagers because it allows them to ask you a question after you ask them one. You can start with statements like these:

- My goal in life is . . .
- I like being (or look forward to being a teenager) because . . .
- I know God is real because . . .
- The person I respect most is . . .
- The reason I respect this person most is . . .
- A good teacher should . . .
- The thing I like best about myself is . . .
- The thing I would most like to change about myself is . . .

What children want most in their parents:

1. Parents who don't argue in front of them.

2. Parents who treat each family member the same.

3. Parents who are honest.

4. Parents who are tolerant of others.

5. Parents who welcome their friends to the home.

• Being a Christian means . . .
• When I am a parent, I will . . .
• The funniest thing that ever happened to me was . . .
• The place I would most like to visit is . . .
• If I had a million dollars, I'd . . .
• What I like best about you is . . .
• My weirdest dream was . . .

A great book to assist in this game is *The Book of Questions* by Gregory Stack, Ph.D. (New York: Worman, 1987).

The Communication Cycle

The first person makes a statement. The second person says, "What I hear you saying is . . ." and then interprets what the first person said. The first person then affirms the interpretation or repeats the statement. Continue until both of you are getting the same message and understand what the other person is actually saying.

The goal is understanding what the other is saying, not necessarily agreeing or putting words in the other person's mouth.

Family Sports Caucus

List as many different sports as you can think of. Use two categories: team sports (softball, soccer, football, basketball, volleyball, hockey, and keep-away, hide-and-seek, and tag for preschoolers) and individual sports (tennis, wrestling, gymnastics, track, swimming, golf, bowling, table tennis, bicycling, ice skating, rollerblading, archery). Talk about which ones the family might be interested in pursuing.

Trying sports as a family provides good initial exposure. It gives your child a chance to try activities without being embarrassed by peers. It can also lead to backyard athletics with friends. It's likely that one thing will lead to another and eventually to competitive sports.

Game Night

After the dishes are cleared and clean, bring out the fun and games!

Board games to consider are

- The Ungame
- Pictionary
- Balderdash
- Monopoly
- Risk
- Jenga
- Trivial Pursuit (We've just discovered the new Eighties Series, and we even know some of the answers!)

Some card games are

- Double Solitaire
- Go Fishing
- Canasta Rook
- Uno
- Hearts
- Crazy Eights
- Rummy

A Puppet Show

Have a puppet show with puppets children made during the week. They plan the show and present it to the parents one evening. See pages 241–243 for ideas on how to make puppets.

*T*reasure Hunt Dinner

What do you do when your spouse is out of town on business and the children are restless? Have a Treasure Hunt Dinner! Divide the food into courses and write unpoetic jingles for each course. Here are two examples:

> "The bananas are where the bandanas are found;
>   Look in the chest and not on the ground!"
> "Carrots are crunchy and have lots of Vitamin A;
>   Search for them where your coats are supposed
>   to stay."

Wrap the different courses of food in plastic bags (if you are concerned about the environment, you might want to put each course in a reusable margarine cup), and hide the courses in the appropriate places along with the next clue. Your clues can lead them through courses of carrots, celery, banana, and raisins, then, finally, to the bathtub for a dip in the "mini-pool."

This last maneuver leaves you time to warm the hot dogs and get out the catsup. With bath time behind them and all the children in pajamas, serve Hot Dogs à la Carte, accompanied by milk in each child's favorite cartoon cup.

After the dinner feast give the children one last clue to lead them to a candy corn dessert. A couple of stories later, bed all the children down for the evening.

Then what? Have a wonderful time just for one! Finish your favorite leftovers—and the candy corn—curled up with a good book.

*F*amily Financial Bible Study

F or a productive Family Night activity, look up verses on earning, giving, saving, and spending, and discuss them with your family. The way you approach this study will depend on the ages of your children and your family style. Consider the following

- Choose one topic, and use this study for four sessions.
- Ask questions to make the verses personal.
    - —What does this verse say to me?
    - —How does this verse relate to our family?
    - —What changes to do I need to make in my own life?
- Write out verses on small pieces of paper and put them in a hat or a jar. Take turns drawing out one verse at a time. Identify whether the verse deals with earning, giving, saving, or spending.
- Identify people who have real needs and discuss how your family can help
- Choose a family project that includes earning, giving, saving, and spending. For example, you could plan a family garage sale. From the amount of money earned, decide how much you want to save, to whom and how much you want to give, and one special thing

you would like to do as a family or purchase for your family.

Here are several verses to get you started. Use a concordance or cross-references to find other verses on these four important subjects.

- Earn:
  Proverbs 14:23
  Proverbs 20:4
  Proverbs 21:15
  Proverbs 24:30–34

- Give:
  Proverbs 3:9–10
  Proverbs 19:17
  Proverbs 28:27
  Luke 6:38
  2 Corinthians 9:6
  2 Corinthians 9:7–14
  Philippians 4:10, 16, 18–19

- Save:
  Proverbs 16:1
  Proverbs 16:8
  Proverbs 22:7
  Proverbs 23:4–5
  Proverbs 30:25

- Spend:
  Psalm 37:16
  Proverbs 30:8–9
  Matthew 6:25–34
  Philippians 4:11–14

"*I*nner Beauty" Discussion Time

P lan a time to set personal goals for inner beauty. The key verse is 1 Samuel 16:7 (TLB): "But the Lord said to

Samuel, 'Don't judge by a man's face or height. . . . I don't make decisions the way you do! Men judge by outward appearance, but I look at a man's thoughts and intentions.'"

Inner Beauty/Outer Beauty

Begin the time together by talking about two kinds of beauty. Identify what makes a person outwardly attractive (good looks, nice clothes, strong body, good figure, etc.). Then help family members define characteristics of inner beauty (love for others, kindness, patience, willingness to help others, etc.). Compare God's statement in 1 Samuel 16:7 with 1 Peter 3:3–4. What do these two Bible passages say about God's view of inner and outer beauty?

Beautiful People We Know

Have family members identify people who have true inner beauty. Decide why family members feel these people have this essential beauty.

Also name two or three people who are attractive from an outer beauty standpoint. Do inner and outer beauty sometimes go together? Why or why not? Can a person be unattractive outwardly but still have real inner beauty? Why?

Enjoying a Family "Beauty Snack"

As you eat, talk about which is best for a person to focus on every day—inner or outer beauty? Why? What would the world be like if everyone focused on outer beauty? Would the world be better or worse if everyone concentrated on inner beauty? Why?

Personal Beauty Plan

Give each person a sheet of paper. Allow time for everyone to write out *one* way he wants to try to be more beautiful in outward appearance. Then each person should plan for at least *two* ways to work on improving inner beauty. Decide together if you want to share your goals or keep them secret as each person's private plan.

Name That Feeling

T ake turns identifying facial expressions. You can make a face and let your child describe it as "an angry look" or "a happy look." You can also look through a magazine and identify feelings of the people you see in the pictures.

Communication Tip of the Week

T ry this fun family venture to improve your communication with each other. Decide on a certain number of communication rules for the same number of weeks: five rules for three weeks, for example. Write the rules on slips of paper and put them in a jar. On a designated day each week, draw out that week's rule. Here are three family-tested examples:

Week One: No "you" statements.
Often, sentences that begin with "you" attack the other person; "I" statements are much safer. They tell your feelings without leveling charges against another person.

"*You* never take the trash out!" "*You* are irresponsible!" "*You* are so messy!"

The first week we tried this communication rule there were a lot of uncompleted sentences, but there were two happier households. We found ourselves beginning to say, "I would appreciate it if you would take out the trash."

Week Two: Express your feelings and really listen to the other person.

Do you know how it is when you want to discuss a difficult issue and you just don't know how to begin? We can get into an argument before we ever get to the issue! This rule has really helped us to get the issue out in the open and attack *it* instead of each other. We begin by stating how we feel. For instance, "I am frustrated . . . disappointed . . . anxious." This helps us state our feelings and our position without attacking.

Week Three: Say positive things!

Every day each family member tries to say at least one nice thing to each of the other members of the family.

When you try to communicate with your teenager, . . . "Talk, don't bug!" . . . "Bugging is when you talk in order to get your kid to do something. Talking is when you don't want anything and you communicate."

*C*ommunication Tennis

W ith a tennis ball in hand, make a statement or ask a question that requires a response. At the same time pitch the tennis ball to your child. She answers your question and then makes a statement or asks a question that requires you to respond and pitches the ball back to you. You may ask, for example, "What do you like about [name a friend at school]?" After your child answers, he may toss the ball back and ask, "What were your friends like when you were my age?" See how long you can keep passing the ball back and forth.

Use this game on Family Night as a good way to help your children initiate conversations with grandparents, relatives, or other adults with whom they have difficulty carrying on a conversation.

*P*uzzle Time

T ry to find a puzzle with diverse people or animals. Once, Claudia and her family put together a puzzle of 501 cats. It was difficult because the cats were so much alike, but each had unique pieces that fit only one unique cat!

As you put your puzzle together, your family can use the time to discover and accept each person's uniqueness by talking about

- How we fit together as a family
- How each of us is a unique "puzzle"—none of us is complete
- The missing pieces and the developing picture— which do you tend to concentrate on in your family?

A word to the wise: Choose an appropriate level puzzle. If your children are small, choose an easy one. If you finish the puzzle early enough in the evening, consider gluing it to cardboard cut to the same size and letting the children use it to decorate the play area.

*F*amily Appreciation Night

G ive each person a card and pencil. For younger family members who aren't old enough to write, oral answers will be fine. Have each family member write down one thing he or she appreciates about each person in the family. Then take turns in sharing your insights with each other. Two kickoff questions you can use are

- What is the greatest strength I bring to our family team?
- What is the one thing I like best about our family?

You will enjoy hearing the positive answers, and your family will be affirmed in the process.

A "Roots" Book

T ake your children on a journey into their own roots. Go beyond slides and tapes by developing your own family "Roots" book. Record in a book the funny sayings of your children, family happenings, interesting news of friends and relatives, and other special events. One mother did this for sixteen years. It will never fail to entertain your family when you review events like these: At five, Mickey seriously thought he could fly and designed elaborate costumes for his attempts; Caroline made up the most fascinating lyrics and once slept in the dentist chair—through three fillings; Kelly very logically announced one day, "I can tie my shoes, bounce the basketball under my knees, and even blow my nose. I must be six instead of four."

Most of us haven't kept a "Roots" book for sixteen

years, but we can begin now. It's never too late to begin cataloging memories! Use a scrapbook, a fancy book, or an old notebook. Assemble several pens, pencils, stickers, and creative minds. Over a couple of Family Nights, ask each child to write down all the clever, ridiculous, happy, and disastrous things she can remember about herself. Then ask each to do the same thing for other family members. Compile the best selections in your "Roots" book, adding appropriate artwork or stickers.

*R*efrigerator Memories

A refrigerator makes a good communication center and catchall for the latest cartoons, snapshots, interesting articles, notes, and children's artwork. Use some magnets, note pads, and a little creativity. When new items replace outdated ones, simply stuff the old ones in a drawer near the refrigerator.

When the drawer is full, take a Family Night to make a Refrigerator Memories Scrapbook. It takes no organizational ability and is just a hodge-podge collection of memories—fun to pull out on a rainy evening and remember how fast the years passed by.

*F*amily Conferences

F amily conferences can make family planning and decision making a lot more fun at your house. Listen to one mom's experience: "We started family conferences when our older child was seven and our younger was three.

Even at those young ages, the children enjoyed them, respected the decisions that came out of them, and learned the basics of leading a meeting in a fun way."

Rules for family conferences can be simple:

1. Anyone can call a family conference, but adequate notice must be given. It is best if they are planned for Family Nights. No one should be forced to cancel previously made plans.

2. All family members must be present at a family meeting.

3. The agenda is open. Each person has a chance to bring up any topic, whether action is needed on it or not. No new topic can be brought up until the one being discussed is completed.

4. The leader for the family meeting rotates. Minutes are kept so that what is decided and who leads the meeting are not in question. (You might want to select a regular minutes-keeper.)

5. Parents have the right to say that a topic may be discussed but is not open to a vote. (This rule comes in handy when children want to discuss chores repeatedly and want to vote that they don't have to do any.)

6. Each person has one vote. Majority rules. Ties mean no action—nothing changes. (If the children outnumber the parents, don't worry. You just have to be careful not to let things that would harm the family come to a vote. For example, you can discuss which child does what chores but not vote on whether or not the chores can be transferred to the parents.)

7. Each person must vote what he or she thinks is best, not what someone else lobbies for. In other

words, family members vote their hearts. No deal making. (That's called political purity.)

After-Dark Secret Pal

A t the beginning of the week, draw the name of someone in the family who will be a secret pal for the week. Encourage everyone to do or make secret surprises for their pal. Be sure that there are some after-dark surprises, like an "I love you" card under a pillow.

Night Lights

Y ou'll need a jar with some grass and a few sticks in it for this adventure—and possibly some insect repellant!

If the mosquitoes are out, you'll need to cover yourself with insect repellant. Poke some holes in the lid of the jar, and venture into the evening to catch lightning bugs.

See who can capture the most in the shortest amount of time. Then discuss what makes the bug light up.

Falling Stars

C all a local wildlife center to find out if they sponsor any evening trips to an observatory.

Or on a clear night you can lie on a blanket and watch for falling stars. Discuss how the stars' light reaches earth and what makes stars fall.

CHAPTER 8

Sick Days

*A*h-ah-ah-choo!"

"Poor baby."

When the flu bug and sniffles invade your home, these remedies are sure to help! Your patient will feel comforted with her own Sick Bell, Patient Chart, and Bedside Companion.

And if the patient is *you,* hand this book to your children and tell them to turn to page 109.

*B*edside Companion

D oes your young child hate being in bed by herself? Make her a companion. Cover a small pillow with an old pillow case, a white towel, or a cloth, and draw a face. Use yarn for hair and buttons for eyes. Now your child has a "companion" to hug and talk to when she is bored.

*T*he "Sick" Bell

E very child (of any age) loves to have a bell by the bed to call the slaves to come when needed. Let family members take turns being on call.

*L*ap Desk

M ake your child a lap desk from an empty packing box. Cut a half-circle in the two long sides of the box and leave the ends as they are. Cover the box with contact paper, or let the child draw on the lap desk and color it. The lap desk will fit nicely over your patient as he sits in bed.

Pencil Box

Make a companion pencil and supply box from a shoe box. Cover it with contact paper. Add pencils, crayons, a small note pad, and anything else you want. I don't know why, but all of our kids loved to play with Band-Aids.™

Sick-Day Drawer or Shelf

In a special drawer or on a shelf, gather supplies for sick days. Books, quiet games, simple craft kits, and a special video or audio tape are appreciated by a child who is under the weather and has to stay at home.

Patient Chart

Pamper your sick child by making his very own health chart on a clipboard. Record temperature and medicine—what was taken and when. You can also record food eaten and liquids drunk. Have a special page where visitors can sign in and out.

*T*ape-a-Book

In your free time (before your child gets sick, if possible), record books on cassettes. For younger children add a "beep" so they can follow along and turn the pages. This will entertain your sick child for short periods of time and give you a break!

*F*amily Photo Show

Let your sick child look through old family photo albums. It will help her remember good times and look forward to fun times in the future.

When a Parent Is Sick...

ray!
Delegate duties according to your child's abilities.

- Sorting laundry
- Doing laundry
- Cooking one dish of a meal
- Ironing
- Setting the table
- Returning phone messages, saying, "My parent is sick and will call you as soon as possible"
- Delivering goodies, magazines, flowers, or medication to the patient

- Sharpening pencils for the patient's crossword puzzles
- Checking on a sibling
- Giving a backrub or backscratch. (There is healing in touch!)
- Plop a card in the mail.
- Hire a housekeeper!

When a Grandparent Is Sick...

P ray!

- Send cards. Make your own or, if you're in a hurry, buy a cheerful get-well card or gift.
- Call! Ask if certain times are good. Is this the kind of illness they'll sleep through or toss and turn through? Do they need company or quiet?
- Bake cookies, make homemade chicken and rice soup.
- Sing songs or read to them. If you play an instrument, give a short concert.
- Write encouraging notes for seven days; ask patient to read one each day.
- Send a tape (see page 250).

When a Friend or Neighbor Is Sick...

P ray!

- Offer to get the mail.
- Offer to take care of pets.

- Offer to grocery shop for a day (or deliver the groceries Mom or Dad has bought and put them away).
- Offer to bring in the paper.
- Offer to babysit.

CHAPTER 9

Getting to Know Me

Yes, families are complex

Yes, parenting is a challenge.

Yes, we need all the help we can find!

This chapter will help you remember that your child is a sparkling, special gift to you from God Almighty. Here are ideas that will help you know and love your complex, challenging, precious child more personally. Intertwined with these ideas are prayers for a richer love within your family.

Helping our children develop healthy self-images cannot be accomplished quickly; it's a continual process of helping our children see themselves as God sees them. But as you apply yourself to some of these projects, it is with the prayer that your children's conclusions to "I am . . ." will be, "I am a child of God. I am happy. I am learning."

Books About Self-image

M any of the books available on the subject of self-image can help us help our children.

Hide or Seek by Dr. James Dobson (Revell) is one we cannot recommend highly enough! Put it at the top of your list of books to read. The book explicitly explains the problem of self-image and gives great encouragement to parents.

Your Child's Self-esteem by Dorothy Corkville Briggs (Dolphin) is another good book for parents. Others include *The Blessing* by Gary Smalley and John Trent (Thomas Nelson); *How to Really Love Your Child* by Dr. Ross Campbell (Victor); *My Book About Me* by Dr. Seuss and Roy

McKie (Random House); and *My Family, Myself* by Carol Batchelor (Hayes). You might also read *Key to Your Child's Heart* by Gary Smalley.

Why I'm Me

Have family members write descriptions of themselves. Then talk about which are inherited traits and which are acquired traits.

A Gift for No Reason

A gift could be some cute stickers, a bucket and shovel, a soccer ball, sunglasses, sugarless gum, or anything (anything cheap, that is!). The gift itself is not important; it's the message: "I love you just because you're you."

You could even get "artsy" and write a poem, like this one that a child found attached to new colored markers:

Because you're special and neat
I bought for you a little treat!
May you have fun as you draw today
And your talents and creativity display!

The poem may not win any literary awards, but the child will delight in her importance.

If poetic ability is not your strong suit, just write a note expressing your love. You can use a small index card, a cute sticker, and a felt pen. It is much cheaper than buying a commercial card. Again, it is not the gift or the poem or a lovely card that is important; it's that you took the time to buy or make a small gift and express your love for your child.

A Positive Log Notebook

Make or purchase a small notebook for each child. On the first page, write your own description of your child's unique personality. On the second page, list unique characteristics of this child for which you are thankful.

Then on the third page, begin a running diary of positive things you observe about your child. Date each entry. You don't have to write something in your notebook each day or even each week, but whenever you observe something really positive or unique about this child, record it.

On the days you are ready to resign as Resident Mom, pull out your Positive Log Notebook and note that tomorrow will probably get better! It will help you keep your perspective.

A Self-esteem Passport for Your Child

Helping your child feel good about himself is not always easy. You might try giving your child a self-esteem passport.

Start by looking at different areas in your child's life. Write down the positive things you see in a "passport."

> Don't be guilty of shooting your own troops with cutting and derogatory remarks! There are enough people out there who will tear us down. Our families need all the affirmation we can give them.

- How is your child an original?
- Has your child recently shown growth in academics? Relationships? Sports or a hobby?
- How has your child shown personal courage?
- How has your child demonstrated self-confidence?
- What other things in your child's life make him unique?

Include your child's picture, and let your child decorate the passport with her original art.

Building our children's self-esteem begins with us but challenges your children! To help them realize confidently who they are and that they are of infinite worth, precious, and capable people, give them appropriate challenges. Encourage them in a given direction—toward wanting to learn, wanting to keep their rooms neat, wanting to make good choices.

These fun ideas provide a challenge that will help develop character qualities in your child. He has fun, and in the process good habits are formed! A challenge may be worked out cooperatively between parent and child. It needs to be achievable and measurable and may include a celebration or reward at completion. Keep the activity simple and under two or three weeks at first.

A Preschool Challenge

A preschooler may learn

- Child and parents' full names
- Address
- Phone number

- ABCs
- Basic numbers
- Colors

As you adopt a preschool challenge, let us challenge you to make it fun and not push your child to excel. Pushing only adds to the child's stress level, and stress is one thing we can all do with less of! For instance, let's take the challenge of learning colors. Why not plan a field trip to a craft or fabric store? Usually you can purchase small, inexpensive squares of felt in many bright colors. Let your child pick colors he doesn't recognize. Later, at home, talk about the names of the colors. You may even want to write the name of each color right on the felt sample. Use a broad-tipped felt marker. After all these colors are mastered, you can repeat the activity.

An Elementary School Challenge

The mother of an elementary school child might help her plan one of the following challenges:

- Read a book of choice and write a book report
- Learn how to sort dirty clothes and operate the washer and dryer
- Select eight or ten key Bible verses and memorize them
- Learn to use a word processor
- Begin keeping a journal
- Read the Bible daily—put a star or check on the calendar each day the Bible reading is completed. Try to read six days each week. Reward biweekly.

- Make a salad or dessert for dinner once a week for three weeks
- Adopt a shut-in from church and visit once a week
- Keep a diary of a special trip or school vacation

A Reading Challenge

Consider these books for your preschooler (2–5 years and older):

- *The Bible in Pictures for Little Eyes* by Kenneth Taylor (Tyndale)
- *The Muffin Family* series (Harvest House)
- All the Arch Books (Concordia)
- *He Is My Shepherd* by David and Helen Haidle (Multnomah)
- *Little Visits with God* by Johsmann and Simon (Concordia)

For a variation, occasionally substitute a video for reading time. A good example is *One-Minute Bible Stories* by Shari Lewis (Sparrow).

Some books for young school age children (ages 6–12 and older) are:

- Their own *The Living Bible*
- *Stories for the Children's Hour* by Kenneth Taylor (Moody)
- *Devotions for the Children's Hour* by Kenneth Taylor (Moody)
- *Treasures of the Snow* and other books by Patricia St. John

- *Alexi's Secret Mission* and other books by Anita Deyneka
- *Sugar Creek Gang* series by Paul Hutchens (Moody)
- *The Sowers* series (Mott Media)
- *The Guessing Books* by Fern Neal Stocker (Moody)
- *The Student Bible* (NIV Zondervan)
- *The Picture Bible* (Zondervan)
- *Beginners Bible* (Queststar)
- *Bible Studies* by Paula Rinehart (NavPress)
  —*Never Too Small for God*
  —*One of a Kind*
  —*Stuck Like Glue*

*H*iding God's Word

To teach the value of memorizing God's Word, challenge your child to memorize two verses each week over a three-month period.

First choose the verses and write them on small cards—or better yet, have the children write them.

Make a case for the memory cards so they can be taken on trips and learned well. Materials needed:

- Felt in two or three colors
- Needle with a large eye
- Yarn in a pretty color

Have the children cut two pieces of felt just a little bigger than the memory cards. Use the yarn and needle to stitch up three sides. Use a color marker to put each child's name on his memory verse case.

You may want to put a sticker on each card with a

verse the child has memorized. Or you may offer a treat for each verse memorized.

A Proverbs Notebook

One of our main goals as parents should be to teach our children to study God's Word independently. The Proverbs notebook is a short-term project to start them on their way.

For one month help your child make and keep a Proverbs notebook. You will need

- 5″ x 7″ notebook (or any size)
- Pen or pencil
- Stickers, if desired, to decorate the pages
- Colored pencils

Challenge your child to

- Read one chapter of Proverbs each day
- Write down in the notebook a favorite verse from the chapter
- Draw a picture with the colored pencils about something in the chapter
- Share the Proverbs notebook with you daily or once a week

A Super Challenge for Parents

This super challenge will help you be good models for your children and, at the same time, encourage them to grow spiritually. There are four basic steps: (1) pray, (2) teach what the Scriptures say, (3) be an example yourself, and (4) take them through the process. You'll see how workable these four steps are as we relate them to planning challenges for our children.

1. *P*rayer

C ommit your way to the LORD, / Trust also in Him, and He will do it" (Ps. 37:5).

- Choose from verses listed in step 2, and pray that they will become real in your children's lives.
- Thank God for healthy bodies, time, and energy for service to others.
- Ask God *specifically* to show you and your children
  —WHO to serve,
  —HOW to serve,
  —WHEN to serve.

> Parents are the bones on which children sharpen their teeth.
>
> Peter Ustinov

2. *T*eaching What the Scriptures Say

I n teaching our children to serve others with their time, abilities, and money, a list of Scripture verses like the ones that follow can help.

Hebrews 13:16	Proverbs 25:21
Isaiah 58:10–11	Acts 20:35
Leviticus 19:32	Romans 12:10

John 15:12	Ephesians 4:32
Matthew 25:40	Philippians 2:3–4
Luke 3:10–11	Proverbs 22:9
Colossians 3:23-24	1 Timothy 6:18
James 2:15–17	Matthew 7:12
Galatians 6:10	John 13:34–35
1 John 3:18	2 Corinthians 9:7

Choose a verse a day. Then discuss what the verses mean and what you can do to apply that verse to your lives.

Children can better apply the verses if they make a notebook, in which they record the verses and then write "what this verse means" and "what this verse means to me," as one child did:

- Hebrews 13:16—"And do not neglect doing good and sharing; for with such sacrifices God is pleased."
    - —What does it mean?—It means we're supposed to do nice things for people and that God likes it when we do nice things and share.
    - —What does it mean to me?—It means I should share my things with others and do good and nice things.
- Luke 10:25–37 (parable of the Good Samaritan)
    - —Ask: What does it say? What does it say to me?
- Mark 12:41–44 (parable of the widow's mite)
    - —Ask: What does it say? What does it say to me?
- Read together, or have your child read alone, a biography of Amy Carmichael. Have your child write a book review about what she learned about sharing with others from Amy Carmichael.

You may also want to try reading and discussing other books or passages with your children.

Younger children can learn valuable lessons by reading the Arch Books: *The Rich Fool* or *The Boy Who Gave His Lunch Away.* Another good selection is Shari Lewis's *One-Minute Stories.*

*3. B*eing an Example

B e sure you are an example of what you are teaching about sharing with others. Remember, the children are always watching!

*4. S*haring the Process

B egin by asking your children for ideas of how they can serve others. If you have studied some of the Scriptures together and talked about sharing with others, they should have lots of ideas. Help them decide which projects are suited to their ages, abilities, interests, and availability. Then walk through the projects with them.

When fifteen-year-old Amy taught a foreign child to read, her parents did not just suggest it and then drop out of the picture. They encouraged their daughter to go to the nearby elementary school and talk with the first-grade teacher about how Amy should teach the young child. The teacher gave her suggestions and books to use. The mother also checked with Amy regularly, and they talked weekly about the child's ready progress. Amy did the weekly training, but her mother was involved in the process with her.

Challenging your children to grow spiritually and

share with others establishes a firm basis for healthy self-esteem through self-mastery and productive connection to others in God's world.

Name Acrostic

To help their children feel special, the Dillows made each of them a name acrostic. With stick-on letters, they pasted their names on pieces of heavy colored paper. Then they took a magic marker and wrote a quality beside each initial:

> **J**oyful
> **O**rganized
> **Y**ourself

To complete the project, the Dillows framed the "artwork" so the children could hang them in their rooms.

CHAPTER 10

Kitchen Capers

*H*ave you ever eaten a Purple Cow? Do you ever hope to eat one? That's only one of the fun-to-make treats you'll find in these pages. Raggedy Ann Salad, Wacky Cake, Breakfast Quickies, and other kitchen capers will delight the eye and the tastebuds. Kids will love to make them—and to eat them. Cooking with your kids can be fun! Try it!

"*Q*uicky" Cooking Tips

S ince we all have to eat and most of us really enjoy it, we'll start with cooking tips. Of course, it is wonderful to bake your own bread and cookies from scratch, but when you don't have the time, consider these tips.

- Homemade bread baking in the oven can make your home smell as if you've been slaving for hours in the kitchen. Simply buy frozen loaves and plop a loaf out to rise as you come in the door.
- You can top pizza dough with ready-grated cheeses and sliced pepperoni. Children love to help "make" their very own personal pizza!
- Another dough tip is to roll the dough out and brush with melted butter. Sprinkle with sugar and cinnamon, roll into a long roll, and cut with a thread. *Voilà!* You have homemade cinnamon rolls that will charm any family member!
- It's amazing what you can do with cookie dough you buy in rolls. Slice, bake, decorate with Red Hots or already prepared icing that you simply squeeze onto the cookies.

The work will wait while you look at the rainbows. . . . Take a cookie break. Don't just bake the cookies. Sit down and eat them together.

Chinese Take-Out

One of our favorite quickies is Chinese take-out food. We set the table with flowers and candles, hide the paper containers, and presto! An Oriental dinner fit for a king or queen. Don't forget the fortune cookies and slices of oranges to top off your delicious meal.

A You-Can-Eat-It Necklace

Give each child a bowl of Cheerios and a bowl of Fruit Loops (or any cereal with a hole in the middle) and a string. Let your children create their own special necklaces. Then, with a glass of juice or milk, let them eat their necklaces. But don't let them eat the string!

Eggs in a Frame

Pull the center from a slice of bread, or cut out the center with a biscuit cutter.

Butter the bread generously on both sides. Brown the bread "frames" on one side in a moderately hot buttered frying pan. Turn over and drop the egg into the center.

Cook slowly until the egg white is set. Cover the pan until the white starts to set.

Sprinkle lightly with salt, and lift out with a pancake turner.

Tuna Delight

Preheat oven to 325°.

1 can tuna
1 can mushroom soup
¼ c. milk
potato chips (about ¾ of a medium pkg.)

Put some potato chips into a bowl. Break them into small pieces by pressing them against the sides of the bowl.

Empty a can of tuna into another bowl. Break up the pieces.

Put the potato chips into the bowl with the tuna. Add the mushroom soup and milk. Mix everything together.

Rub butter or margarine around the inside of a baking dish.

Pour the tuna mixture into the baking dish. Bake in the hot oven for 30 minutes.

Surprise Sherbet Sandwiches

Two hours before serving, spoon orange or lime or rainbow sherbet into a six-ounce orange juice can. Cover the top with aluminum foil, and freeze the sherbet for two hours. Remove the foil and the other end of the can. Push out the sherbet and cut it into eight ½″ slices. Put each slice on the back side of a round butter cookie. Top with another cookie.

Serve surprise sherbet sandwiches on the most boring

day you can find. Preferably, it should be a day when the kids have moped around the house, are lazy bums, and finally ate breakfast at 11:00 in the morning. An hour after their late breakfast, when they have finally gone outside to play, go to the door and sternly call them in for lunch. You will probably hear complaints: "I'm not hungry." "We just ate breakfast." "I don't want anything to eat!"

Respond with, "Well, that's just too bad. It's lunch time, and I've made your sandwiches. You have to come in and eat two sandwiches each before you can play any more!"

As the children grudgingly come to the table, serve sherbet sandwiches and watch the amazed smiles and laughter break out on their faces. You'll find that once again you have chased away boredom and one more boring day has been transformed into fun memories. Try it and prove us right. You can be a lazy-day star at your house.

*P*izza Muffins

Margarine	*Knife*
1 pkg. English	*Broiler or toaster oven*
muffins, split in	*Cookie sheet*
half	*Frying pan*
1 8-oz. can tomato	*Wooden spoon*
sauce	*Can opener*
½ lb. ground beef	
1 4-oz. can	
mushrooms	
2 T minced onions	

1 t. oregano
½ t. garlic salt
1 pkg. sliced
    mozzarella cheese

Lightly toast buttered muffin halves on cookie sheet under broiler. In frying pan, brown meat and pour off grease. Add mushrooms, sauce, onions, and seasoning. Let cook down until it is "sloppy Joe" consistency. Put a heaping spoonful on each muffin half. Top with a slice of cheese and run under the broiler for 1 minute.

Watch carefully. Makes 8 small pizzas.

*F*ruit Pizza

F ruit pizza? It's yummy!

Preheat oven to 325°.

Crust:
1 c. butter
1 c. sugar
2 c. flour

Cream butter and sugar and slowly add and mix in flour. Press into a 12–14″ pizza pan (or whatever you have that will work). Bake for 35 minutes. Cool.

Topping:

8 oz. cream cheese	1 T honey
1 t. cinnamon	½ t. vanilla

Cream these items together and spread the mixture over the cooled crust.

Arrange assorted fruits (strawberries, kiwis, peaches, etc.) over the filling. Glaze with a cup of apricot or peach preserves, thinned with 2 T of water. Chill and serve in wedges.

A Snowman Cake

Grease and flour two round layer pans, one 8″ by 1½″ and one 9″ by 1½″. Prepare any flavor cake mixes as directed on the package, divide the batter between the two pans, and bake.

On a foil-covered cardboard, place the smaller layer for the snowman's head and the larger one for the body. Using a white frosting mix, frost the layers, joining them together. Sprinkle with flaked coconut.

Use semisweet chocolate pieces for buttons; gumdrops for eyes, eyebrows, and the nose; red shoestring licorice for the mouth; and red rope licorice for the muffler. Place a large chocolate wafer cookie on each side of the head for earmuffs.

While the cake is baking, the kids can make their own paper snowflakes (see p. 58).

*P*eanut Butter Krispies

½ c. sugar   *½ c. light corn syrup*
2 c. Rice Krispies   *1 c. peanut butter*

In a medium glass bowl, stir the sugar and corn syrup. Microwave on high for 3 minutes or until the mixture comes to a full boil. Stir in the cereal and peanut butter. Drop teaspoonfuls of the mixture onto wax paper.

Cookie Surprise

This one's really easy! Just hide a roll of slice-and-bake chocolate chip cookies in the freezer. When boredom or the blues strike, just take out, slice, and bake to restore smiles.

Purple Cows

1 c. grape juice
1 scoop ice cream
½ c. milk

Blend juice, milk, and ice cream in a blender.

Chocolate Peanut Butter Sticks

8 oz. semi-sweet
*   chocolate chips*
1 t. vanilla

6 T peanut butter
1 c. wheat germ

Melt chocolate chips, and blend with peanut butter and vanilla. Stir in the cup of wheat germ. Press the mixture into a greased 8″ square pan, and chill until firm. Cut into bars.

Wacky Cake—Extra Simple!

Preheat oven to 350°. Into an ungreased 12″ by 12″ pan, mix the following, sifted together:

1½ c. flour   *1 t. soda*
1 c. sugar   *½ t. salt*
3 T cocoa

Make three holes in these dry ingredients. Into one put 6 T vegetable oil. Into one put 1 t. vanilla. Into one put 1 T vinegar.

Then pour 1 cup cold water over all and stir with a fork until smooth. Bake for about 30 minutes.

Frosting
2 c. powdered sugar   *1 t. vanilla*
2 T cocoa   *3 T cold liquid coffee*
½ c. melted margarine

Mix all ingredients together, leaving the coffee until last, and pour on *hot* cake.

Treasured Balls

This one is simple but fattening.

Preheat oven to 350°.

1 c. margarine
6 T brown sugar
1 T vanilla

1 c. semi-sweet
   chocolate pieces
2 c. less 4 T sifted
   flour

Soften the margarine. Add brown sugar and vanilla. Cream. Add semi-sweet chocolate pieces. Blend in flour.

Shape into 1″ balls. Bake on ungreased cookie sheet 15–20 minutes. Cool and roll in powdered sugar.

Molasses Cookies

Preheat the oven to 350° for this easy roll-out cookie for advanced beginners.

1 c. margarine
1 c. sugar
1 c. molasses

2 t. soda
4 T milk
4½ c. flour

Melt margarine and mix with sugar and molasses. Sift dry ingredients and add alternately with milk to molasses mixture. Chill and then have fun rolling out! Bake on greased sheet until done (about 8–10 minutes).

Lunch Helper

You and one child can create a lunch for family members who are home. The lunch doesn't have to be fancy.

It can be the old standbys—peanut butter and jelly, tuna, grilled cheese, or egg salad sandwiches. The point is to do it together and to spend the time alone with one child. Allow extra time to share and talk and to have your child help.

If you want to add a gourmet look to your luncheon or are just in the mood, try Bologna and Cheese Animal Sandwiches. They are perfect for an indoor lunch or a picnic in the backyard. To make them, cut out bologna, cheese, and bread with animal cookie cutters, and stack. Serve with carrot sticks, chips, and milk (served with straws, of course!).

Send-a-Dough Cookies

S end a "cookie-dough" gift through the mail. Do you know a child in your town or another town who is confined indoors due to illness, or a child who just needs extra caring? These "Send-a-Dough Cookies" are perfect! Your child makes the dough, packages it, and mails it. The receiver adds a few ingredients and presto! Send-a-Dough Cookies are made! This recipe is for two batches—you can send both or send one and keep one.

2½ c. flour	1½ c. shortening
1 t. baking soda	3½ c. quick cooking
1¼ t. salt	oats
1 c. sugar	1 c. raisins
1 c. packed brown	1 c. chocolate chips
sugar	

Stir together the flour, soda, and salt; stir in the sugars. Cut in the shortening until it is thoroughly blended. Thoroughly stir in the oats. You'll have about 10 cups.

Measure half of the mix (about 5 cups) into a plastic bag. Add ½ cup chocolate chips and ½ cup raisins. Close the bag tightly. Put the remaining mix, raisins, and chocolate chips into another bag and close tightly.

To mail: Use a container that can be sealed up well, like in a plastic bag, then a box. Include the following instructions on how to bake!

Beat together 1 teaspoon vanilla, 1 teaspoon water, and 1 egg. Stir into the dry mix. Drop spoonfuls of batter onto a greased cookie sheet and bake at 350° until golden brown.

Here are some slow-cooker recipes that you can start in the morning before you leave for a busy day.

Time goes, you say? Ah no!
Alas, Time stays, *we* go.

Henry Dobson
The Paradox of Time

*B*elieve It or Not—Chicken in the Pot

1 3-lb. chicken, whole or cut up	2 t. salt
2 carrots, sliced	½ t. coarse black pepper
2 onions, sliced	½ c. water or chicken broth
2 celery stalks, with leaves, cut in 1" pieces	basil to taste

Put carrots, onion, and celery in the bottom of the crockpot. Add the whole chicken or chicken pieces. Top with salt, pepper, liquid. Sprinkle basil over the top. Cover and cook on low setting until done, 7 to 10 hours. Serves 4–6.

Serve this dish with fresh fruit yogurt salad. Cut your favorite fruits—or those you have on hand—into bite-size pieces and use your favorite fruit yogurt as dressing for a yummy salad.

Swiss Steak

> 2 lbs. round or Swiss
> steak cut ¾" thick
> Salt and pepper to
> taste
>
> 1 large onion, sliced
> thin
> 1 1-lb. can tomatoes

Cut the round steak into serving pieces; season with salt and pepper, and place in the slow cooker with sliced onion. Pour tomatoes over all. Cover and set on high for 1 hour and turn to low for 8 to 10 hours.

Creamy Swiss Steak

F ollow the recipe for Swiss Steak (above), substituting 1 can of mushroom soup and ½ can of water for tomatoes. Spread the soup evenly over the top. Both of these recipes are delicious and take only minutes to prepare.

Here are two ideas for fun cooking days with the kids.

Raggedy Ann Salad Luncheon

In the morning gather your crew for a creative time in the kitchen. Choose one of the simple cookie recipes below to bake, and make Raggedy Ann Salad for later in the day.

Easy Peanut Butter Cookies

Preheat the oven to 375°.

1 c. peanut butter	1 egg, beaten
1 c. sugar	Believe it or not, there is no flour.

Mix the ingredients together and drop by spoonfuls onto a cookie sheet. If you prefer, shape the dough into balls and pat down with a fork. Bake for 10 minutes.

Sugar Cookies

Preheat the oven to 350°.

1 c. sugar	½ t. cream of tartar
¾ c. salad oil	½ t. soda
1 egg, beaten	½ t. salt
2 c. flour	½ t. to 1 t. vanilla

Mix sugar, oil, and egg. Sift together the dry ingredients and combine with the sugar mixture. Mix in the vanilla, roll the dough into balls, and flatten the balls a little. Put them on a cookie sheet and flatten them with a fork, criss-crossing the fork design. Bake for 10 minutes. Sprinkle the tops with sugar.

Raggedy Ann Salad

Body	*Fresh or canned peach half*
Arms and legs	*Small celery sticks*
Head	*Half of hard-cooked egg*
Eyes, nose, shoes, buttons	*Raisins, nuts*
Mouth	*Piece of cherry, a red hot, sliver of grated carrot*
Hair	*Grated yellow cheese or carrot*
Skirt	*Ruffled leaf lettuce (with tuna hidden under skirt if desired*

Enjoy a wonderful lunch together. The children may want to make place cards for the table or have candles to make it special. After lunch, take a nature hike around the neighborhood—a good way to work off cookie calories. Give each child a bag and let her collect leaves, wildflowers, weeds, stones, mosses, and other collectible treasures. If you feel extra creative, upon returning from the neighborhood hike, provide glue and paper, and let the children shape their collected "treasures" into a nature-hike collage.

*M*ake-Ahead Mixes

One of the fun—and useful—things to teach our children is how to plan ahead. On this cooking day the children will make two mixes that they will be able to use several times.

For lunch you can use part of the bran muffin batter

and serve the muffins fresh from the oven with butter and honey. Cook Tuna Patties, a children's favorite. The Frosted Fruit Cocktail will go in the freezer to be used the next day and the day after.

Six-Week Bran Muffins

These healthy muffins taste good for breakfast, lunch, or dinner.

Preheat the oven to 350°.

3 c. All Bran cereal	*2 eggs*
1 c. boiling water	*2½ c. flour*
½ c. margarine	*2½ t. soda*
½ qt. buttermilk	*1 t. salt*
¾ c. honey	

Bring the water to the boiling point; add shortening and All Bran. Set this mixture aside to cool, or cool it with the buttermilk. Beat the honey and eggs together and add to the All Bran mixture. Add the buttermilk now if you didn't use it to cool the hot mixture. Bake in greased muffin tins for 25 minutes. You may use it all at once or store the batter in the refrigerator for up to six weeks. Yields 36 muffins.

Frosted Fruit Cocktail

This concoction can be used as salad, dessert, or base for punch. It's perfect on hot summer days. And it keeps forever in the freezer.

> 3 medium bananas,
>   mashed
> ½ c. sugar (can be
>   omitted)
> 1 c. crushed pineapple
>   in heavy syrup (use
>   fruit and juice)
>
> 2 lemons, juiced and
>   strained (or ⅓ c.
>   lemon juice)
> 2 c. orange juice
> 2 c. ginger ale or
>   Sprite

Mix these ingredients in the order given. Freeze the mixture in a clean ½-gallon milk jug or other container. Take out of the freezer about ½ hour before serving. Serve in bowls when slushy. Return unused portion to the freezer.

To use this fruit cocktail as a punch base, put the frozen mixture in a large bowl, let it thaw some, and then pour 3 to 4 bottles of ginger ale over it, stirring some to break up the frozen mixture. Best punch we've ever had!

Tuna Patties

This is a children's favorite to fix alone when Mom and Dad are out on a date.

> 1 7½-oz. can tuna
> 10–12 Ritz crackers
>
> 1 egg
> Salt and pepper

Drain the tuna and then mix all the ingredients in a bowl. Form into three patties and fry them in a small amount of oil until brown on both sides. Serve with catsup!

CHAPTER 11

Holiday Helpers

*H*ave you occasionally found yourself in a "holidaze," needing a nap more than you need a celebration? The holiday suggestions in this chapter can help you to make lasting family fun memories and avoid the "holidaze." But be forewarned! Don't try to do all these activities in one year. Pick and choose what suits your family this year, and save the other activities for future holidays.

So go ahead and celebrate the Fourth with a birthday cake for America, have a brown-bag Christmas party, and hide thrill-and-fill eggs this Easter. We guarantee fun for your family now and for years to come!

The Pilgrims publicly said thank you to God for the harvest and for their safety. Here are some practical ways we can express our thanks on Thanksgiving and all through the year.

"*I*'m Thankful for..."

Together as a family, make a thankful list. Take turns adding to it. Start with the youngest family member and work up to the oldest. See how many things and experiences you can name.

Post your list on the refrigerator, the bulletin board, or wherever your communication center is. Date and save the list as a record of some of the things the Lord has done in your family.

A Thanksgiving Prayer

Have someone in your family write out a special prayer to share at your Thanksgiving dinner.

*T*hanksgiving: An Answered Prayer Bowl

D uring the year as you and your children observe ways God answers prayers, write each answer on a piece of paper, fold it, and put it in a special bowl. You may want to keep this bowl in the dining room or somewhere you will see it often. Then as a Thanksgiving tradition, take turns reading the answered prayers during your Thanksgiving dinner.

The Thanksgiving holiday is well established—but are thankful hearts a vital part of the Thanksgiving tradition at your house?

*T*hanksgiving: A Cranberry Symbol of a Peacemaking Time

F or the Pilgrims, Thanksgiving was a time for peacemaking. Cranberries—one of our traditional Thanksgiving foods—symbolized peace among early Indian tribes. The story goes that the Indians presented the Pilgrims with gifts of cranberries as a sign of friendship and peace.

With a blunt needle and coarse thread, string cranberries. Put the string on a tree in your yard for the birds.

*T*hanksgiving: Peacemaking Practice

A s a family take a few moments to thing about people in your lives who are not easy to get along with. Talk about how the Pilgrims and the Indians made peace. Think about how different they were from each other and how that would complicate things. Then think of at least one nice thing you can do for someone who is hard to get along with.

Life-Size Indians and Pilgrims

U sing a large piece of paper, trace around your young child. Newsprint is great to use; tape two sheets together if necessary.

Let the child color and decorate the outline as a Pilgrim or an Indian. Cut out the Indian or Pilgrim and put it on the wall.

Ask your child, "Who do you identify with more—the Indians or the Pilgrims? Why?"

Thanksgiving: Sharing in a Mayflower Basket

T he Pilgrims were generous and shared their blessings with others. How can you and your family share with others this Thanksgiving? Consider a Mayflower basket.

Let the children decorate a basket. Fill it with goodies that an elderly friend could use:

- Canned food
- Fruit
- Nuts
- Bottled water
- Stationery
- Stamps
- Assorted cards (birthday, get well)

Take the basket to an elderly friend or neighbor. Put the basket on the doorknob or by the door. Ring the doorbell and hide!

*T*hanksgiving: A Pineapple Turkey

A special way to say "I'm thankful for you" to a teacher or special friend is to give a pineapple turkey. Mr. Turkey makes a quick and easy centerpiece, and he's practical—he may be eaten later.

Mr. Turkey's head is simple to make for anyone learning to sew.

Materials:

- One fresh pineapple with bushy leaves
- Popsicle stick
- Thread
- Felt (brown red, white, and black)
- Scissors
- Glue

Push the Popsicle stick firmly into the bottom of the pineapple. Assemble the turkey head and neck as you see here, and place it over the stick.

*T*hanksgiving: Adopt a Family

T hink about a family you know that has special needs at this time of year. If you don't know such a family, check with your church, the Salvation Army, or a local welfare agency. Invite your adopted family for Thanksgiving din-

ner. In December you can provide toys and other gifts to
help make their Christmas special.

Thanksgiving: Helping with a Feast for the Poor

As a family, volunteer to help with cooking and serving
Thanksgiving dinner for the poor. Check with local welfare agencies, the local rescue mission, or the Salvation
Army. While you would probably not do this every year,
it is a great experience for your family to have at least
once.

Thanksgiving: Cook-Together Time

Thanksgiving is a great time to include your family in
the preparations. One mother in a PEP Group for Moms
shared that she lets each child choose one dish to make
for Thanksgiving dinner. She does as much preparation
as possible ahead of time—usually the day before.

Even a simple contribution will help the child feel included. One year this mom's five-year-old son got excited
about fixing beans! With Mom's help he opened the can
of green beans and "cooked" them in the microwave. Because they were sharing Thanksgiving dinner with a
family across town, they put the beans in a dish, stored
them in the refrigerator overnight, and took them to the
family Thanksgiving dinner the next day. Yes, they had

to reheat the beans—but her son was so proud and actually ate them too!

Her other son chose to make gumdrop bread. "It tasted awful," she said, but the children loved it. Should you want to try something so exotic, here's the recipe.

Thanksgiving Gumdrop Bread

¾ c. tiny gumdrops
3 c. flour
¾ c. sugar
1 T baking powder
1 egg

¼ t. salt
1⅓ c. milk
⅓ c. cooking oil
½ t. vanilla

Preheat the oven to 350°. Generously grease a loaf pan.

With kitchen scissors, cut the gumdrops in half. (If your scissors start sticking together, dip the blades into a glass of cold water.)

Put the cut gumdrops into a large mixing bowl. Add the flour, sugar, baking powder, and salt, and stir with a wooden spoon until well mixed. Set this mixture aside until you're ready to use it.

Crack and beat one egg in a small bowl. Add milk, oil, and vanilla. Beat until well mixed.

Pour the egg mixture into the flour mixture. Stir until the dry ingredients are wet. The mixture should be lumpy, so don't stir too much. Put the mixture into the greased loaf pan. With a rubber scraper, scrape the bowl and spread the mixture evenly in the pan.

Bake for 60 to 65 minutes. To see if the bread is done, push a wooden pick into the bread near the center. If the pick comes out dry, the bread is done.

Set the loaf on a cooling rack. Run a metal spatula around all four sides of the pan. Turn the pan on its side. Shake the pan gently to remove the bread. Set the pan aside, and turn the bread right side up. Cool the bread completely before cutting. Makes one loaf.

*T*hanksgiving: Cornucopia Place Cards

o add a festive atmosphere to your Thanksgiving celebration, let your children make unique place cards.

A clever place card can be made with colored construction paper, one Bugle™ (a horn-shaped corn snack), glue, and small dried flowers or weeds. Baby's breath works well.

Cut the construction paper into pieces 3″ by 4″. Fold each in half lengthwise. Glue one Bugle™ on each card. Fill the Bugle™ with dried flowers, and glue them in place. Write a name on each card with a felt-tip pen. Presto! You have unique place cards for the Thanksgiving dinner table.

*T*hanksgiving Acrostic

he acrostic activity from page 126 can be adapted for any occasion. One year, for example, when the Dillows celebrated Thanksgiving, they made a placecard for each person at the table. The word *Thanksgiving* was turned into an acrostic, which had esteem builders for each person:

> ROBIN is
> Thoughtful
> Helpful
> Animated
> Nice
> Kind
> Silly
> Genuine
> Interesting
> Vivacious
> Intelligent
> Nifty
> Giving

The children's placecards were framed to be hung on the walls in their bedrooms.

All you need is heavy paper for the cards, press-on letters, magic markers, and small frames, if desired.

Thanksgiving: A Time for Considering Your Heritage

One Thanksgiving the Arps were guests in the home of a large family. As we all sat around the table, our hostess asked who could tell the story of the first Thanksgiving. Piece by piece, the story began to emerge—part fact and part fiction. Amidst the laughter we realized that it is up to us as parents to pass down the heritage and history of Thanksgiving.

Thanksgiving Reading

R ead the Thanksgiving story to your children. Books suggested by mothers are

- *The First Thanksgiving Feast,* Joan Anderson (New York: Clarion/Ticknor & Fields, 1984)—an easy reader
- *Thanksgiving Day,* Robert M. Bartlett (New York: Crowell Jr. Books/Harper Jr., 1965)
- *How Many Days to America?* Eve Bunting (New York: Clarion/Ticknor & Fields, 1990)
- *Arthur's Thanksgiving,* Marc Brown (Boston: Little, Brown, 1985)
- *Thanksgiving at the Tappletons,* Elie Spinelli (New York: Trophy/Harper Jr., 1989

The following books are available from Oleanna Books, Box 141020, Minneapolis, Minnesota 55414:

- *My First Thanksgiving Book,* Jane B. Moncure
- *Squanto and the First Thanksgiving,* Joyce K. Kessell

Noticing God's Bounty

V isit your local farmers' market or grocery. Point out which fruits and vegetables are harvested in each season, and appreciate the colors, textures, and shapes of the bounty. Maybe try something new for dinner.

*L*ooking Ahead—Making an Advent Wreath

A dvent begins four Sundays before Christmas and goes through Christmas Eve. Some calendar years, the first Sunday of Advent is the first Sunday after Thanksgiving, so this is a timely activity. Let us encourage you to make Advent a time of getting hearts and homes ready for the celebration of the birth of Christ. To make Advent more meaningful for your family this year, make an Advent wreath.

To make a wreath choose a circular base of Styrofoam™, wire, or wood, with holes for four candles (the circle represents eternity). Attach evergreen branches— real or artificial—to the base (evergreens stand for everlasting life and hope). Add pine cones, holly, or other decorations.

Insert four candles for the four Sundays of anticipating Christmas, and put a large candle in the center of the wreath to represent Christ, the Light of the world.

Light one candle on the first Sunday, two on the second Sunday, and so on. As the candles' light grows brighter each week, so will your desire to celebrate the coming of Jesus—the Light of the world.

*C*hristmas Nightgowns

E ach year Grandmother makes "all the same" nightgowns for the women and girls in the family. What a special memory—lovely new nightgowns every Christmas, their similarity binding each woman and girl into the family.

A Birthday Gift for Jesus

A nother family told us, "We sang 'Happy Birthday' to Jesus and talked about what we wanted to give to Him. Then we decided on a private gift, something of ourselves to give to Him. We wrote it on a piece of paper and tied it to the Christmas tree. After dinner we lit the lights on the tree, turned out the other lights, and prayed together as a family. This tradition helped to bring the true meaning of Christmas on Christmas Eve before the presents on Christmas morning.

"As the children grew older, singing 'Happy Birthday' to Jesus was definitely not on their 'cool' list of things to do, but some traditions can continue, like having a special Christmas Eve dinner, praying together for each family member's goals for the new year, and celebrating together. Traditions change with our families, but we continue to make memories."

Simplifying Traditions—

- Cooking
- Shopping/Gift giving
- Activities calendar

We've provided a blank calendar for you, plus a sample, on pages 158–159. Plan wisely.

December

Behold, what manner of love the Father has bestowed on us, that we should be called children of God!–1 John 3:1

SUN	MON	TUE	WED	THU	FRI	SAT
		27 Family Planning. Discuss what we'll do, what we won't do.	**28** Set up Christmas Factory (with wrapping supplies).	**29** Pull out Christmas decorations!	**30** Hang Advent Calendar.	**1** Draw names for Advent Secret Pals. Do 1 kind deed a day until Christmas.
2 Light 1 Advent candle Read Isaiah 9:2, 6 John 8:12	**3** Set up Nativity Scene.	**4** Family Night Make your own Christmas cards.	**5** Give a compliment!	**6** Read the story of St. Nicholas.	**7** Draw names for stockings. Set $10 limit. (For families with older kids)	**8** Create 'n Bake Day!
9 Light 2 candles Read Luke 2:4–7	**10** Open Christmas cards together. Pray for each family.	**11** Make someone smile.	**12** Read aloud as a family.	**13** Get in shape! Exercise as a family.	**14** Make a snowman (If no snow use styrofoam & cotton balls).	**15** Invite someone who lives alone to dinner.
16 Light 3 candles Read Luke 2:8–14	**17** Count your blessings!	**18** Take holiday lights tour of your community.	**19** Call someone you rarely see.	**20** Light tree & candles. Play Christmas music & be silent 10 minutes.	**21** Make gifts-of-love coupons (babysit, yardwork, shop, etc.).	**22** Celebrate 1st day of winter with cookies & hot chocolate.
23 Light 4 candles Read Luke 2:15–20 John 1:1–12	**24** Light 4 candles; then light the Christ candle. Read Luke 2:1–20	**25** Take turns opening gifts. Celebrate His Birthday!				

After-Christmas Tips:
• Put together a Christmas puzzle.
• Take a "group nap" around the Christmas tree.
• Watch a football game (if you must!).
• Enjoy your family—now!

December

SUN	MON	TUE	WED	THU	FRI	SAT

Consider making some of your gifts. You don't have to be a great cook, seamstress, or crafts person to make a personal, thoughtful, meaningful gift. Many times it is simply a matter of putting several items together and tying them up with a cute ribbon. Here are some suggestions of homemade gifts you can make with your children.

Spiced Tea

Combine

> 1 large jar of Tang™
> 1 large package
>   Country Time
>   Lemonade™

> 1 large jar sweetened
>   and lemoned tea
> Ground cloves to taste
> 3 T cinnamon

Mix and fill containers. Decorate with a bow or tree ornament.

Seasoned Salt

> 1 box iodized salt
> 1½ oz. black black
>   pepper
> 2 oz. red pepper

> 1 oz. garlic powder
> 1 oz. chili powder
> 1 oz. Accent™

Combine and place in a bottle or jar with a tight-fitting lid. Makes 32 ounces. Divide into small jars for gifts. Baby food jars are a great size.

*F*estive Apple Bread

Preheat the oven to 325°.

1 egg	*1½ c. plain flour*
1 c. butter	*1 t. cinnamon*
Dash of salt	*2 c. fresh apples*
1 t. baking soda	*(diced)*

Mix all the ingredients. The batter will be thick. Bake it in foil loaf pans for 45 minutes. You can also bake it in miniature loaf pans. Give the bread and the pan as a gift.

*S*pool Candlesticks

Buy spools at an antique market. Add candles and bows. They cost about three dollars each.

*C*innamon Baskets

Use an orange juice can, a rubber band, ribbon, and cinnamon sticks. Cover the can with cinnamon sticks, using the rubber band to hold the cinnamon sticks in place. Tie with festive ribbons. Fill with pecans, cashews, or peppermint candy.

*F*ragrant Pomander Balls

1 orange
1 small box of whole cloves
Colored ribbons

Tie the ribbons around the unpeeled orange so that the fruit is quartered, with ribbon ends streaming down. Pin the ribbon in place. Press the cloves, stem first, tightly together into the orange until the fruit is covered. Tie a handling ribbon from the top. The cloves will preserve the orange. As it shrinks, it gives off a festive aroma. Tighten the ribbons after one week.

A Photo Album for Grandparents

I f you have cleverly saved negatives of your favorite candid family snapshots, have copies made for a special album for grandparents.

If you are like our families and have no idea where the negatives are, you can take your color pictures to a quick print shop and have color copies made. You may be amazed at how nicely they turn out. This process is also great when you need the pictures immediately. Usually there is no waiting, and you can go home with your color copies.

*C*oupons of Service

E ach coupon may be cashed in for certain activities or things you know the recipient would appreciate. The best gifts don't have to cost a lot of money. Sometimes the best gift is the gift of ourselves. Possible coupon service gifts are

- Babysitting
- House cleaning
- Baking a favorite dessert
- Teaching a child how to build a birdhouse
- Setting the table each evening for a week

*G*oody-of-the-Month

G ive older family members and friends who don't need more "things" a Goody-of-the-Month certificate. Each month you or your child can prepare a different "goody" and deliver it with a personal visit.

*I*nexpensive Gifts

W hat about gifts for nieces, nephews, cousins, and other friends? Realistically, you can't make them all, so here are suggestions from others of what's current today.

Gifts are great to get, but much more important is the time you spend with your family building relationships.

Games—Always Great Gifts

Consider these:

- Hot Potato—This is a simple one, but you get to throw this stuffed potato around, so it's a crowd pleaser.

- Pictionary Junior Play It with Clay—This guess-the-word game is just like its cousin except that you use clay to make the clues.
- Domino Rally—You set the plastic dominoes up and watch them tumble down in patterns.
- Slap Happy—Each child gets a huge, brightly colored foam hand, and you see who can slap the right color dot first.

Puzzles

Berenstein Bears, Duck Tales, Where's Waldo?, and lots of puppies and kittens for little children. One set that looks wonderful is My First Giant Jigsaw Puzzle. The puzzle of Big Bird has nine pieces and is twenty-one inches tall and fourteen inches wide when completed.

Other Inexpensive Gifts

- Koosh balls—Even kids who already have some seem to want more. They come in all sizes.
- Play-Doh Fingles—These little kits give you the fun of Play-Doh without the whole factory. You mold finger puppets in the molds and can then play with them. For ages four and up.
- Rug hooking kits—Children ages six to twelve can make small rugs in a variety of designs with these kits.
- Pottycraft—Air-dry clay makes this a good gift for the artistic child in the family. You get three pounds of air-dry clay, enough to make a pot or vase, and it doesn't have to be fired. Paint and glaze are included.

Stocking Stuffer Name Draw

For families with older children, put everyone's name in a hat—parents included—and draw names. Each person is responsible for stuffing the stocking of another family member. Set a price limit like ten dollars per stocking.

A Bank for Jesus

Six weeks before Christmas begin a bank for Jesus. The whole family saves money during the six weeks. They decide on a Christmas project that would please Jesus.

One family used the bank money to buy gifts for children who were spending Christmas in the hospital. The gifts were small magic markers and coloring books, tablets of paper, and so on. The whole family wrapped the gifts and took them to the children in the hospital.

Christmas Countdown Chain

Cut different colors of construction paper into strips 1″ by 6″. Write a number on each from 1 to 25. Then make a chain by gluing the strips together in the correct order. Hang the chain in a prominent place (like in the kitchen) and let children take turns tearing off one loop each day.

As a variation make a Countdown Calendar and open a door each day. Or hang little goodies on a crafted tree or Velcro™ them onto a decorated felt calendar.

A Christmas Factory

C hoose a special room or corner in your home where you can keep supplies for wrapping gifts and creating Christmas specials. Possible supplies include paper, ribbon, tape, scissors, Styrofoam™, glitter, glue, buttons, stickers, a glue gun, boxes, and so on.

For money-stretching packaging suggestions, consider these:

- Plain brown bags with burlap ribbon, twin, or red and green yarn. Add Christmas symbols or holiday greetings with felt-tip markers or stencils.
- Newspaper for large packages. Children love getting the comic sections.
- Pine cones, evergreen sprigs, or tiny tree ornaments on packages
- Gift tags made from recycled Christmas cards

Chrismons for the Tree

O ne of several decorating ideas the whole family can do, Chrismons (Christian monograms) are Christian symbols that have been passed down through the years. Following are various patterns for ornaments for your Christmas tree. You can cut the Chrismons out of Styrofoam™. Spray or outline them with glue. Decorate with gold or silver glitter.

The Latin cross symbolizes the type of cross on which Christ was crucified.

The fish was a sign used by early Christians. The letters IXΘΓΣ form an acrostic on the Greek phrase "Jesus Christ, Son of God, Savior."

> *"But these are written that you may believe that Jesus is the Christ, the Son of God, and that believing you may have life in His name" (John 20:31).*

The first and last letters of the Greek alphabet stand for Jesus Christ.

> *"'I am the Alpha and the Omega, the Beginning and the End,' says the Lord, 'who is and who was and who is to come, the Almighty'" (Rev. 1:8).*

The circle and triangle represent the eternity of the Trinity.

> *"For there are three who bear witness in heaven: the Father, the Word, and the Holy Spirit; and these three are one" (1 John 5:7).*

The scroll symbolizes the Pentateuch, the Law, the first five books of the Bible.

> *"Do not think that I came to destroy the Law or the Prophets. I did not come to destroy but to fulfill [it]" (Matt. 5:17).*

The lamp symbolizes the Word of God.

> *Your word is a lamp to my feet*
> *And a light to my path. (Ps. 119:105)*

"There shall be no night there: They need no lamp nor light of the sun, for the Lord God gives them light. And they shall reign forever and ever" (Rev. 22:5).

The descending dove with a three-rayed nimbus (halo) around its head is a symbol of the Holy Spirit.

"When He had been baptized, Jesus came up immediately from the water; and behold, the heavens were opened to Him, and He saw the Spirit of God descending like a dove and alighting upon Him. And suddenly a voice came from heaven, saying, 'This is My beloved Son, in whom I am well pleased'" (Matt. 3:16–17).

The cross and crown symbolize that Jesus Christ is King of kings and Lord of lords.

"He humbled Himself and became obedient to the point of death, even the death of the cross. Therefore God also has highly exalted Him and given Him the name which is above every name, that at the name of Jesus, every knee should bow, of those in heaven, and of those on earth, and of those under the earth, and that every tongue should confess that Jesus Christ is Lord, to the glory of God the Father" (Phil. 2:8–11).

Dough Christmas Ornaments

Preheat oven to 300°.

Mix together
2 c. flour
1 c. salt
1 c. water

Knead together. Roll out and cut with cookie cutters. Brush with beaten egg. Punch a hole at the top of each ornament before baking.

After baking and cooling, push red and green yarn or ribbon through the hole and make a tie for each ornament. Leave the ornaments natural or paint them with acrylic paints. Spray varnish for a lovely finish.

*I*ce Cream Cone Christmas Trees

You will need

- Cone-shaped ice cream cone
- Can of frosting
- Blunt knife
- Assortment of small candies and sprinkles (Red Hots work great!)

Stand the cone point up for a tree shape, ice with frosting, and decorate with candies and sprinkles.

*C*hristmas: A Yearly Family Scrapbook

Designate December as scrapbook month. Save all your favorite snapshots through the year. Pull them out in December and make a scrapbook of your year. It's also the time to pull out scrapbooks from previous years and enjoy the memories of years gone by. In one family we know, making the scrapbook is Dad's special job.

A Visit to a Christmas Tree Farm

Plan a visit to a Christmas tree farm and cut down your own tree! If they sell evergreen wreaths, think about buying one for your children's bedroom doors. They can even decorate them if they want.

Caroling

Organize a choir of family and friends and go Christmas caroling! Call ahead to alert your neighbors to the fun! At the end of the evening celebrate with hot chocolate or hot spiced cider, sugar cookies, and the Christmas story by the fire.

Christmas Read-Alouds

Read *The Littlest Angel* by Charles Tazewell and *The Little Drummer Boy* by Ezra Jack Keats. They illustrate the true meaning of giving.

Christmas Ornament Collectibles

Make a Christmas ornament that your child can take with him when he is grown and starts his own home. Initial and date the bottom, and hang the ornament on the tree. Keep a separate box for each child's Christmas collectibles.

A Snowman Without Snow

A re you sad that you don't have a white Christmas? That won't stop you from making a snowman! Use cookie dough, cotton balls, or Styrofoam™. Definitely use your imagination!

A Christmas Holiday Tour of Lights

T ake a tour of your community after dark. Let the kids plan the route. If you are really energetic, make it a walking tour.

*S*traw in the Manger

A ssemble your nativity scene at the beginning of December. You might want to set up two nativity scenes, a china one to "look at" and one that your children can hold and touch. This activity is for the nativity scene that you can touch.

Leave the manger empty and have a small container of straw nearby. As each child does something she feels is loving and kind, she adds a straw to the manger. On

Christmas Eve or Christmas Day, when baby Jesus is laid in the manger, your children will appreciate that their kind deeds helped to prepare His bed.

*B*rown-Bag Party

Liberality consists less in giving a great deal than in gifts well timed.

Jean de la Bruyere
Les Caracteres,
Du Coeur

Have an impromptu brown-bag Christmas party. Roll down the tops of brown lunch bags, and fill each bag with goodies to munch around the tree. You could use nuts, dried fruit, popcorn, miniature muffins, and cookies. Put on your favorite Christmas tape, light the tree, and take a few minutes to enjoy each other and the magic of this time of year.

*B*irthday Cake for Jesus

Bake a birthday cake for Jesus, and share it on Christmas Eve or Christmas Day. Before you sing "Happy Birthday" to Jesus and blow out the candles, explain the symbolism to your children:

- White, round cake for Jesus' purity and for His eternal reign.
- Twenty candles for the twenty centuries since Christ's birth. Red candles for the blood Jesus shed for us and for Christmas joy. Lighted candles to remind us that Jesus is the Light of the world.
- A silver star in the center for the star of Bethlehem (can be made with silver candles or by covering cardboard with aluminum foil).

• An angel in the center for the first angel who told the good news of Jesus' birth.

*C*hristmas: Scripture Names of the Lord

Take turns looking up the Scripture passages and reading

• Matthew 1:16	Christ
• Hebrews 6:20	High Priest
• Acts 2:32–36	Risen Lord
• Exodus 3:14	I Am
• Acts 20:28	Shepherd
• John 3:2	Teacher
• John 1:41	Messiah
• Revelation 3:14	Amen
• John 20:31	Son of God
• Isaiah 9:6	Wonderful Counselor, Mighty God, Everlasting Father, Prince of Peace

*C*hristmas: Ten Minutes of Silence

Each evening before bedtime, gather around the tree. Light the tree and perhaps candles as well. Turn out the electric lights, play Christmas music, and observe ten minutes of silence. This is a wonderful way to "soothe the

wild beast," and bedtime will be much calmer and more pleasant.

*H*oliday Stress Busters

THE CHRISTMAS LAMENT

Two days before Christmas and all through the house,
There is so much to do, I feel like a louse.

The stockings are hung all over the chair;
The clothes are all dirty; there's nothing to wear.

The kids are not sleeping, but fighting instead;
It looks like me and Pa will never get to bed.

The cookies need baking; there's shopping to do.
If Christmas is so great, why am I so blue?

When it's time for you to take a mini-break and try some stress relievers, consider one of the following ways to give your body a chance to relax:

- Take a warm bath to calm you by increasing circulation and relaxing muscles.
- Breathe deeply. When the heart is racing with anxiety, breathing deeply will help you relax. Take a walk around the block.
- Build a fire, turn on soft music, and have a cup of hot chocolate or hot tea.
- Sing your favorite Christmas carols—to yourself.
- Have a quiet time. Read your favorite Scripture passage or read Psalm 2:3.
- Keep your sense of humor.

- Write in a journal. Sometimes summing up the day's or week's highs and lows helps you to laugh at them and keep things in perspective.

Celebrating Christmas Afternoon

Take time to wind down as a family. Each year we have a Christmas puzzle that we begin to put together on Christmas afternoon after all the celebrating is over.

Also consider pulling out the sleeping bags and taking a family nap around the Christmas tree. It's time to relax!

Seven Days to Easter

Starting on Palm Sunday, follow Jesus' footsteps. Choose an unhurried time when the family can be together each day, possibly in the evening before bedtime or right after dinner. Each day, read the appropriate Scripture passage. Discuss what you read and talk about the objects listed.

Day 1—Palm Sunday

Subject:	Jesus entering Jerusalem
Scripture:	John 12:12–19, Mark 11:1–11
Objects:	Palm branch or other greenery
	Donkey

For young children: Let's have a parade. Pretend Jesus is coming to town. Make banners; blow up balloons. Pull out the rhythm band and have a parade!

Day 2—Monday

Subject: Jesus at the temple, turning over money changers' tables

Scripture: Mark 11:15–19, Matthew 21:12–17

Object: Coins

Day 3—Tuesday

Subject: The withered fig tree, prayer, faith, forgiveness

Scripture: Mark 11:12–14, 11:20–25; Matthew 21:18–22

Object: Fig tree, figs (Use another kind of tree or fruit if you want; you could substitute dates or apricots.)

Day 4—Wednesday

Subject: Woman anointing Jesus; Judas agreeing to betray Him

Scripture: Mark 14:1–11; Matthew 26:6–13, 26:14–16

Objects: Perfume (Pour some on felt.)

              Thirty silver coins (nickels, dimes, quarters, play money)

Day 5—Thursday

Subject: The Lord's Supper, foot washing, Garden of Gethsemane

Scripture: Mark 14:17–26, 32–42; John 12:1–17

Objects: Cross, crown of thorns (made from a rose bush)

              Dice, sponge, nails

Day 6—Friday

Subject:	The Crucifixion; the burial
Scripture:	Luke 23; Matthew 17:1–61
Object:	Cross, crown of thorns (made from a rose bush)
	Dice, sponge, nails

Day 7—Saturday

Subject:	The tomb; prophecy of Crucifixion
Scripture:	Matthew 17:62–66; Isaiah 53
Objects:	Stone
	Lamb
	Tomb

Scripture:	The Resurrection, the empty tomb
Subject:	Matthew 28:1–5; Luke 24:1–49
Objects:	Angel
	Bread

Depending on the ages of your children, use the objects in one of the following ways:

- Cut the objects from felt and use them on a felt board.
- Hide the objects for the day, and let your children hunt and find them.
- Use things you can find around your home, displaying them on the table as you have your discussion.
- Talk about each object, and let the children draw and color it.
- Encourage your children to come up with other symbols that remind them of Easter.

To make your time together special, light a candle. Talk about how Jesus is the Light of the world.

Dyeing Eggs Together as a Family

The custom of exchanging eggs began before the birth of Christ. The Egyptians and Persians dyed eggs in spring colors and gave them to their friends to celebrate new life.

The early Christians were the first to use colored eggs at Easter. Later, in Europe, Christians colored eggs red to represent the shed blood of Christ and the joy of the Resurrection.

The tradition of writing messages and dates on eggs began in England. Fancy candy eggs with windows and tiny scenes inside were popular gifts in the 1800s.

For us today, dyeing and decorating eggs can become an opportunity to teach our children of new life offered by God in Christ. Consider some of the following activities.

Hard cook the eggs before dyeing them. Let the children write messages or draw pictures or use Easter stencils on the eggs. Use tape if you want to have two-tone eggs. Be creative and have fun.

An Easter Egg Tree

For the tree, use a branch just as it is or spray paint it white. You can also use sprigs of pussy willow or forsythia blossoms. Put them in a vase or container, and you have an Easter egg tree all ready for decorating.

Make your own egg decorations. Use real eggs. Punch a small hole in both ends of the raw egg. Use an ice pick to break the yolk. Holding the egg over a bowl, blow on one end. With a little effort the yolk and white of the egg should be forced out the other end and into the bowl. (This is a good evening to have omelettes for dinner.)

Paint the eggs any colors that you like. Place the eggs in an old egg carton and let them dry. You can use acrylic or oil paint. Decorate any way you want. You can paint designs on the eggs—hearts, flowers, or curlicues. You can use rickrack, borders, stencils, yarn, felt, or whatever you like. You could even cut out little pieces of felt and make an empty tomb on an egg.

Cut the yarn into eight-inch lengths. Thread the yarn through a large needle and tenderly push it through the two holes in each egg. Tie a large knot in the end at the bottom so the yarn will stay and not pull through. Use the other end of the yarn to tie the egg onto the tree.

*F*ive Special Easter Eggs

A nother fun Easter activity is to fill plastic fill-and-thrill eggs with symbols of Easter. Let the children take turns opening the eggs and telling about the symbol inside. You share last, and save one egg that is completely empty. Talk about the empty tomb.

- Yellow = light—On the outside stick a sticker of either a candle or the sun. On the inside place a little scroll with this Scripture: "I am the light of the world" (John 8:12). Also include a little surprise such as an eraser shaped like a candle or light bulb.

- Purple = royalty—Put a crown sticker on the outside. On the inside, a Scripture scroll with 1 Timothy 6:15: "The King of kings and Lord of lords." A surprise could be a crown pin or ring.
- Pink = love—Outside stick a heart and cross sticker; inside, a Scripture scroll with John 3:16, "For God so loved the world that He gave His only begotten Son," and a surprise of a cross pin or ring.
- Green = new life—Put a butterfly sticker on the outside. Inside put a Scripture scroll with Romans 6:4: "Just as Christ was raised from the dead by the glory of the Father, even so we also should walk in newness of life." Add a surprise, anything with a butterfly on it (for instance, a pin or ink stamp).
- Blue = peace—Outside stick a dove sticker. Inside put a Scripture scroll with Isaiah 9:6, "Prince of Peace," and a dove pin.

Most of these stickers and little gifts can be found at a Christian bookstore.

*E*aster Story in an Eggshell

You can recreate the Easter story, showing, an empty cross, or Christ on the cross with one of the people who was there watching.

Supplies needed:

- Large white plastic egg (Pantyhose eggs work well.)
- Easter basket grass
- Popsicle stick broken into two pieces and glued in cross shape

- Baby doll to represent Christ (You can make one out of a tiny ball of fiberfill covered in nylon hose and wrapped in blue fabric. Draw on a face with a pen, and use yarn for the hair.)
- Tiny artificial flowers
- Ribbon, lace flowers to decorate outside of egg

*E*aster Cookies

Make rolled cookies and cut out as crosses, flowers, candles, eggs, lambs, and empty tomb. Decorate.

See recipe on pages 138–139 or use rolls of dough.

*A*n Easter Banner

Make an Easter banner for your door. Use a large, vertical piece of felt or plain paper. The title could be "He Is Risen." Your child could then illustrate the Easter story: a cross, the empty tomb, the angels, the excited disciples, or whatever reminds him of the Easter story.

*I*ndoor Easter Lily Garden

Plant lily bulbs in a pot and watch them grow as Easter approaches. Explain to your children that as bulbs bring new life, Jesus brings new life in our hearts. When we ask Him to live in our hearts, He throws away our bad ways and gently cleans our hearts so He can fill us with brand-new love for Him and people. He gives us a fresh start.

*B*unny Bait

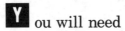 ou will need

- Orange cellophane (available at most paper/stationery shops)
- Candy corn
- Green yarn
- A black pen that will not smear

Place some candy corn in the middle of the cellophane and roll it up in the shape of a carrot. One end should come to a point; tie the other end with green ribbon. Write "Bunny Bait" on the "carrot" and leave in a basket for the Easter Bunny.

*H*ot Cross Buns on Good Friday

Ingredients:

*2 pkgs. active dry
   yeast
½ c. warm water
¾ c. scalded milk
½ c. salad oil or
   melted shortening*

*⅓ c. sugar
¾ t. salt
½ to 1 t. cinnamon
3 beaten eggs
⅔ c. currants
1 egg white*

Preheat oven to 375°.

Soften the dry yeast in warm water. Combine milk,

salad oil, sugar, and salt; cool to lukewarm. Sift 1 cup of the flour with the cinnamon; stir into the milk mixture.

Add the eggs. Beat well. Stir in softened yeast and currants. Add the remaining flour or enough to make a soft dough, beating well. Cover the dough with a damp cloth and let it rise in a warm place until it doubles in size (about 1½ hours). Punch it down. Then turn it out on a lightly floured surface. Cover it and let it rest 10 minutes. Roll or pat it to ½ inch. Cut it in rounds with floured 2½″ biscuit cutter. Shape the rounds into buns. Place them on a greased baking sheet about 1½ inches apart. Cover and let rise in a warm place until almost doubled (about 1 hour).

Cut a shallow cross in each bun with sharp scissors or a knife. Brush the tops with slightly beaten egg white. Bake the buns 15 minutes or until done. Cool slightly, and frost, with icing made from the recipe below. Makes about 24.

Icing for Hot Cross Buns:

Add about ¾ c. powdered sugar to remaining egg white. Drizzle the frosting onto the crosses.

As you enjoy eating the Hot Cross Buns together, talk about how the cross reminds us of Christ's death on the cross and about the yeast as a symbol of new life.

> What will a child learn sooner than a song?
>
> Alexander Pope
> *Epistle,* Book II

*E*aster Music

E ach year teach your children one new Easter song, such as "Christ the Lord Is Risen Today." Talk about the meaning of the song. For young children who can't read the hymnal, it will be fun for them to learn the words that are being sung.

At home, preschoolers enjoy singing and acting out the Easter song "Christ Arose." As you sing quietly and slowly, "Low in the grave He lay," squat down. Then jump up as you loudly sing, "Up from the grave He arose!"

Grandparents' Day

Make Grandparents' Day cards to deliver or send. If you are without grandparents, adopt an elderly friend or neighbor, or call a local nursing home for ideas.

Presidents' Day

Read *Abraham Lincoln* by D'Aulaire. This may be too lengthy for your smaller children, but Mom can glean information and choose pictures. Also try *Presidents of the United States* by Cornel Adam Lengyel for super pictures of former presidents.

Valentine's Day

Surprise your child with "heart" food during the week! Make sandwiches, cookies, pancakes, toast, hamburgers, pizza, melon slices, etc., in the shape of a heart.

And don't forget your mate. You can get ideas from *52 Dates for You and Your Mate* by Dave and Claudia Arp (Thomas Nelson).

*F*lags for the Fourth

Make flags using construction paper, popsicle sticks or dowel rods, red and blue crayons, star stickers, etc. Display them on your door, in your neighborhood celebration, or at your local parade.

*F*ourth of July Picnic with a Flag Cake

Pack a picnic supper and a quilt and go see a fireworks display. You might take along a birthday cake for the United States of America. Ice a rectangular cake with cool whip, and arrange blueberries and raspberries in an American flag design.

CHAPTER 12

Travel Fun

*U*nless you are in the minority, your plans this year will include at least one car, plane, or train trip with your children. Whether you're heading out to visit grandparents, Disney World, or uncharted waters, you know there will be hours of real family togetherness. These traveling tips will help you still love each other after the trip is over!

A Travel Notebook

Have your children make travel notebooks, a great activity for elementary-school-age children. Buy a looseleaf notebook, dividers, and paper. The various sections of the notebook for our pretend trip will be

1. Interesting facts—about Texas, New Mexico, Arizona, California, Indian reservations, or the Grand Canyon. Using an encyclopedia or library books, each child will write information on one of the above topics and share it with the family. This will help them all be better prepared for the trip. They may even make some contributions to the trip itinerary.

2. Travel log—Here the child can write a brief daily diary of the trip.

3. Postcards—The blank, unlined paper in this section is ready for pasting in interesting postcards gathered on the trip.

4. Quiet time—Here the child can record special verses or prayer requests each day. It's also a good place for recording observations on the new beauties and

curiosities of God's world that the child notices along the way.

5. Money—The child can keep an account of his own money and how it disappears!

6. Blank—This children's choice section is filled with blank sheets of paper for drawing, playing tic-tac-toe, or anything the child desires.

You can plan a Travel Notebook Day a few weeks before your summer trip. Begin the day buying notebooks, dividers, paper, and writing utensils. You can take the children to the library to research and write down interesting facts; they can continue this project at home. In the afternoon or evening you can bring out the new notebooks and set up the divisions to get the Travel Notebook ready for use.

*M*y Own Bag (ages two and up)

T hink ahead about your trip—where you will be traveling and what you will be doing. All of this helps you to plan. But no planning is complete without "bag" assembly time.

The bag can be bought or made. It can be an old purse or a plastic sack. One mother's "bag" idea was a metal cake pan with a sliding cover. She said it was an excellent container for pencils, paper, crayons, books, and activity books. And the top doubled as a writing surface.

Another clever mother used paper bags and let her kids decorate two bags each. If you decide to do this you might encourage each child to decorate the second bag as a surprise for one of the other children.

The important thing, though, is that each child have

her own bag (cake pan or whatever!) with appropriate items for her age level. Some bag filler ideas are

- Paper tablet
- Colored pencils
- Colored markers
- Coloring book
- Dot-to-dot book
- Activity book
- Sticker book
- Sewing cards
- Magic slate
- Small cars
- Transparent tape
- Pretty stickers
- Band-Aids (an amazingly popular item that will reveal your child's inventiveness)
- Books
- Favorite stuffed animal or doll
- Scissors
- Flashlight and extra batteries (a fun toy and security in a strange bedroom)
- Card games
- Glue stick (not gooey glue)

Fill your children's bags with items they already enjoy plus one or two new treasures, but most new travel treasures should come from Mom's Surprise Bag.

*M*om's Surprise Bag

A surprise a day keeps tears and quarrels away—at least some of the time! It also adds an air of expectation

to each travel day. Designate a special time each day—two or three in the afternoon is usually a time when travelers begin to feel grumpy and weary of sitting—for the ceremony of the day's treasure.

What treasures does Mom store in her surprise bag? They can be big or small, expensive or cheap, wrapped or unwrapped, something to play with, to make, or to eat. The selection is limited only by your creativity and budget. An important ingredient is that the surprise is right for the age and ability level of your child.

Some sample surprises are

- Hook rug kit
- Sugarless gum (a whole pack for each child)
- Flashlight and batteries
- Books
- Comic books
- Leather-working kit
- Tapes with music
- Magic erasable slate
- Sewing cards
- Colored pencils and paper
- A new pencil and eraser
- Cute pad of paper
- Activity books
- Punch-out paper dolls
- Transparent tape
- Small toy
- Bag of balloons
- Deck of cards
- Doodle art
- Magnetic chess or checkers set
- Needlepoint or cross-stitch kit
- Mini-Mastermind
- Trouble Bubble
- Travel Bingo

Anything listed under My Own Bag is perfect for Mom's Surprise Bag too. Although children love to get sweets, we've found activity-oriented gifts the best as they give the children something to do. You can collect bargain surprises throughout the year for the surprise bag, so they will always be on hand for impromptu trips.

One mom added this tip—for games, check out the birthday party favors at your favorite toy store. Kids love that junk, and it's fairly inexpensive.

A note of warning! When choosing surprises, remember that marbles roll, crayons and chocolate melt, chalk crumbles, bubble gum gets stuck in hair, and small toy parts get lost.

Mom's Own Bag

We've planned for the children—their own bags and Mom's Surprise Bag full of goodies that will warm their hearts and possibly help them sit still. Now, Mom needs a bag for Mom. Begin with a "surprise" for you—a new book or whatever you'd like. then add the essentials for triumphant travel.

- Paper towels
- Pre-moistened towelettes
- Band-Aids
- Jump rope for exercise while stopping for gas, etc.
- Timer for changing seat assignments
- Water jug and paper cups
- Large and small plastic bags (for garbage, motion sickness, laundry, wet bathing suits, etc.)

Food Bag—A Must!

Whether you are traveling by plane, bus, car, or train, eating will be a major activity. Regardless of the games or activities you plan, food will be a star attraction. *Be prepared!* Food requests often come fifteen minutes after you leave home. Chips, candy, cookies, and all the "junkies" will, of course, be well received, but first think about protein snacks and fruits such as

How dear to this heart are the scenes of my childhood, When fond recollection presents them to view!

Samuel Woodworth
The Old Oaken Bucket

• Hard-cooked eggs
• Cheeses
• Raisins
• Nuts (A mix of peanuts, almonds, and raisins is often a favorite.)
• Peanut butter, to spread on crackers, bread, bananas, or celery
• Carrot and celery sticks (immersed in cold water for a long trip, otherwise just washed and packed in a plastic bag)
• Apples, oranges, tangerines, and bananas
• Granola bars
• Gorp (a mixture of peanuts, raisins, and M&Ms)
• Mixture of sunflower seeds, peanuts, and raisins
• Sunflower seeds

To avoid messes and disagreements, try putting combo mixes like the raisin-peanut-almond mixture in individual plastic bags. Popcorn is also a favorite, packed for each child in individual bags.

The Food Bag must also have drinks! One wise mother (not popular, but wise!) carried only ice-cold water while traveling. Spilled, it wasn't sticky and it didn't stain. Since water is less appealing than sweetened drinks, it was requested less often, and subsequent potty stops were fewer. But if you're feeling especially generous, here are some more exciting drink suggestions:

- Small individual cans of juice (frozen ahead and allowed to thaw along the way to be served deliciously ice cold)
- Tupperware plastic glasses with spill-proof lids, filled with juice or just ice cubes that will melt along the way and provide ice water
- Thermos or camper canteens for each child (then they decide when to have a drink and are not constantly saying, "Mommy, I'm thirsty").

*T*he Music Machine

A nother planning tip is to consider incorporating music into your summer trips. Favorite songs sung together make distances seem shorter and give enjoyment to all. Why not take a couple of songbooks on your next trip and learn new songs as you travel?

Today most cars come equipped with a tape deck, but if yours doesn't have one, consider taking a cassette recorder and tapes. Tapes of children's songs are perfect for those times when everyone is all "gamed out" or "sung out" and there are still many miles to go.

Our friends with young children recommend

- Glad tapes
- Integrity tapes
- Psaltry tapes
- *Patch the Pirate* (*Patch* tapes can be ordered from Musical Ministries, Inc., P.O. Box 6524, Greenville, SC 29606).
- Wee Sing tapes

One young mother suggested starting an informal "lending library" among friends. "It's easy to spend ten dollars for just one tape," Cary said. "Before we take a trip, I visit my friends and borrow books and tapes that my children haven't heard. I offer to loan our tapes and books to other families. I'm helping others while modeling to my own children the importance of sharing. It also really helps our limited budget."

You might also carry along a blank tape for taping your family's singing or recording your own stories. Or bring tapes on which you have already recorded some family favorites. Most children will thoroughly enjoy tapes of *Black Beauty* and *Treasure Island*. Even the adults enjoy hearing the stories again and again, and they enjoy even more the silence and absence of bickering when all ears are listening.

Travel time will be wonderfully different (even fun!) when you plan ahead. Taking time to assemble all the bags will make you as prepared as a good Girl Scout. Helping your children make a Travel Notebook will improve their spelling, writing, research, and organizational abilities, and it will probably add an air of excitement about the trip.

We all have our bags, and our children have their notebooks, but now the trip has begun and we must all sit for eight to ten hours a day. *Help!*

A Structured Day

P articularly helpful with younger children is to add structure to your long days of travel. A typical structured day might be:

9 A.M.   Read a Bible story or Christian book to children

10 A.M.   One parent in back seat, if possible, to play a game with children

11 A.M.   Cassette time—if possible, let children use the recorder by themselves.

12 P.M.   Lunch

1 P.M.   Children's games alone or with parents (lots of ideas below)

2 P.M.   Mom's Surprise Bag, play with surprises

3 P.M.   Parent or older child reads aloud from a book— several chapters each day at this time

4 P.M.   Snack time

5 P.M.   If you still have miles to go, turn on the soothing music and pray!

Of course the day can have as little or as much structure as you feel your children need. Variety and structure help keep the children's minds and hands occupied so you hear less frequently, "When will we be there?"

If you run out of games to play, try some of these:

Name That Tune
(ages three and up)

One person hums the melody or claps out the rhythm of a song, and the other players must guess the song. Even very small children can play this game if simple songs for children are chosen.

Collecting Your Years (ages four and up)

The players decide on an object—a church, a train, a certain kind of car. Each player has to find as many as she is years old—four for a four-year-old, eight for an eight-year-old. Everyone who finds his number is a winner!

Silly Stories

Each player tells one line or one paragraph of a story. You make it up as you go along and continue it as long as you like.

Poor Puppy (ages three and up, but best for younger children)

One player, the "puppy," makes faces or funny noises. One at a time the other players pat the puppy on the head and say, "Poor Puppy" three times without laughing. If the "patter" laughs, she becomes the puppy.

Four Is the Score (ages six and up)

Player one says to player two, "Name four rivers." If he can't, the first player has another turn. She then asks player two to name four of something else (cars, states, cities, trees, names that begin with K). When player two can name four, it's his turn to ask for four. Each player who asks for four things must be able to name them himself. If he asks for four of something that he can't name, he loses his next turn.

*E*lf Hide-and-Seek (ages three and up)

P layer one says, "I'm an elf, only three inches tall. Where am I hiding?" The other players have to guess where someone three inches tall could be hiding. "In the Food Bag?" "No." "In Daddy's pocket?" "Yes." The next elf can be two inches tall or any size she chooses.

*M*acaroni (ages four and up)

T hink of something you like to do, like swimming. The other players have to guess it. They ask you questions, and because they don't know your word, they have to use the word *macaroni* instead. For example: "Does everybody macaroni?" "No." "Have you ever macaronied?" "Yes." "Do you macaroni outside?" "Yes." The questions go on until somebody guesses that "macaroni" is swimming.

*Q*uaker Meeting (ages three and up)

N obody talks, giggles, or makes a sound. First to do so loses. (This is a short but effective activity when the noise level has become unbearable!)

*R*oad Map Charting
(ages eight and older)

Give each child a road map of the route you are traveling. As you travel, have them mark your route with highlight markers to help the driver check his progress.

*R*ecord Keeper
(ages eight and older)

Children can become involved in keeping records, and they also can learn a great deal about math without realizing it. They can record

- Number of miles traveled in an hour, a day, or the whole trip
- Amount of gasoline used, cost, and miles per gallon
- Meals eaten and their cost

*A*cronyms (ages eight and up)

The letters on license plates sometimes spell words—especially now with the popularity of vanity tags. Or they can be arranged to spell words. Or they can be acronyms: HTC = High Tension Cable; GOG = Good Old Goat; WSM = Wow! Super Mom!

New Name Game
(ages three and up)

The players all decide on a new name. for the next sixty miles each player *must* be called by his new name. If a player forgets and uses a real name, a point is scored against him. The winner is the person with the lowest score at the end of the sixty miles.

Alphabet Trip (ages five and up)

One player begins by saying something like, "My name is Allison. I'm taking a trip to Africa, and I'm going to bring back some animals." All the words start with *A*. The next player uses the letter *B* and says something like, "My name is Bob. I'm going to Bangladesh, and I'm going to bring back some bottles." All the players take turns, using different letters of the alphabet. Leave out the difficult letter *X*.

Stinky Pinky (ages eight and up)

This is a fun rhyming word game that will help the miles go by quickly. It is a great game for older children and adults. The little tots enjoy listening and taking their turns too—although with them the rules must be modified or ignored.

One person thinks of two words that rhyme, like "green bean." Then two clues are given. The first clue is the number of syllables in each word, which is where the name of the game comes in. If the mystery words have two syllables each, then it is a "stinky pinky." If the mystery words have only one syllable each, it is a "stink pink." Three syllables each makes it a "stinkety pinkety."

If one person has chosen "green bean," he would first give this clue: "I'm thinking of a stink pink."

The second clue is two words that describe the hidden words. For "green bean," the clue could be "colored vegetable," so the person would say, "I'm thinking of a stink pink, and it is a colored vegetable." Then the others must guess until someone comes up with the correct rhyming words, "green bean." Let the person who guesses it right have the next turn, or take turns in rotation.

Think up your own combinations, or use the ones below to get you started. Before the trip, you could write them out on slips of paper, fold them, and put them in an envelope for the children to draw from when they say, "We're bored. What can we do?"

Stink Pinks	*Clue*
roast toast	cooked bread
dumb gum	unintelligent chew
fox box	animal container
hi bye	hello, so long
silk milk	fabric drink
hot pot	heated utensil
heard bird	singing robin
top pop	great dad

Stinky Pinky	*Clue*
able table	capable furniture
hour flower	timed plant
better sweater	improved wrap

Stinkety Pinkety	*Clue*
concentration education	focused learning

Roget's New Pocket Thesaurus can be a valuable aid in this game. Why not stick it in Mom's Bag?

"*I* Remember"

T hink back on the day's activities and try to remember everything possible. Take turns and try to see who can continue the longest remembering things and places visited. This little game will help the children remember and record the things they have seen and done in their travel logs.

When Beached, Build a Castle!

M any learning times are planned at home, but don't fail to take advantage of all the opportunities that trips and travel afford during the summer. On your next visit to the beach, take time to read together the story about houses built on sand and on rock (Matt. 7:24–27). When the tide is out, build a sand castle below the high-tide line. Beside your sand castle pile a few heavy rocks. Then watch what happens when the tide comes in. Share ideas on how this illustrates Jesus' story. Help your children identify Jesus as the "Rock." Let them know that you trust Him because He is dependable and a safe foundation for life.

Memory Mural

To avoid the post-vacation blues when you and your crew make it safely back home, try this project.

After vacation time has come and gone, make a Memory Mural of your trip! Using butcher paper, have the kids draw, paint, or collage a mural of all the family fun. Display it proudly in your kitchen or on a large bulletin board.

Triumphant Traveling

As you, along with families all over America, hit the vacation trails committed to having family fun (no matter how much pain and suffering it entails), your hours in the car, train, or planes can be triumphant! Remember to be prepared, which means to *plan*.

Researching and making Travel Notebooks builds enthusiasm. Mom's bags keep boredom and hunger away. Children's bags add variety and provide a handy place for collecting surprises and souvenirs; music soothes; structure adds sanity; and games are just plain fun! With these tips applied, you just might agree that traveling with children can be fun!

CHAPTER 13

Party Time

*F*our words children love to hear are "Let's have a party!" Parties come in all shapes and sizes. Here are some suggestions for making your next party the best yet!

A Backyard Circus

This is great for a birthday party or a no-reason-at-all party. It may require two days—one to plan, make invitations, and prepare; and one for the actual party.

Remember that tiny tots tire easily, so we need to consider their endurance level (and Mom's too). Mornings are the best times for little ones, so plan activities for early in the day. Toddlers may enjoy a special event in the morning and a nap in the afternoon (maybe for Mom too).

Planning and Preparation

Have on hand the following:

- Balloons
- Washable color markers
- Animal cookies
- Large boxes (from grocery store)
- Finger paint
- Wallpaper scraps, contact paper, etc.
- Cake mix
- String
- Ice cream cones

Make an invitation list. A good rule of thumb is to have a helper (older child, teen, or other mom) for every five children. Also keep the circus party to no more than an hour and a half—for instance, from ten to eleven-thirty.

For invitations, write on an inflated balloon and let your child decorate with color markers. Let the air out and send or deliver in the neighborhood. Be sure to tell each prospective guest to dress as a favorite circus performer and to bring a favorite wild, stuffed animal friend.

Clown Cupcakes

Sure to be a hit at any circus party are Clown Cupcakes! We suggest making the cupcakes the week before and freezing them. Then the morning of the party decorate them with your children's help—or let them decorate them with your help. Use your imagination or the following recipe.

Bake 1 package (18.5 oz.) any flavor layer cake in paper baking cups. Cool.

Prepare butter cream frosting.

⅓ c. soft butter or margarine	1½ t. vanilla
3 c. powdered sugar	About 2 t. milk

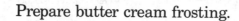

Blend butter and sugar. Stir in vanilla and milk. Beat until smooth and/or spreading consistency.

Frost tops of half of the cupcakes. Remove the paper cups from the remaining cupcakes and frost the sides of each. Invert on the frosted cupcakes and frost the "tops."

To make the clowns, use a pointed ice cream cone on each cupcake for a hat, coconut for hair, sliced almonds or raisins for eyes, and red cinnamon candies for nose and mouth. Insert small candy wafers for ears. Makes 15 clowns, but this does not mean you must have 15 children.

Paintbrush Cookies

Start with your favorite sugar cookie recipe rolled and cut but unbaked, or packaged, unbaked refrigerator cookie dough. You can also use packaged animal crackers, but the "paint" recipe is a little different.

You will also need as many cups and small paintbrushes as you have colors.

Preheat the oven to 400°.
To make the paint for four colors, you will need

> 2 egg yolks
> ½ t. water
> Food coloring

Blend egg yolks and water together. Divide into cups and add food coloring. Use small, clean paintbrushes to paint the unbaked cookies. Add more water if "paint" becomes too dry. Bake for 6–8 minutes, or as directed on recipe.

CAUTION: Don't let the children taste the unbaked "paint" because of concerns about salmonella in uncooked egg.

If you want to use no-bake paint on animal crackers, make the paint with evaporated milk, a little sugar, and food coloring. Allow the cookies to dry before eating them.

Circus Train

Decorate large cardboard boxes as cages for transporting "wild" stuffed animals. Almost anything can be used to decorate—finger paint, color markers, tempera paints, leftover pieces of wallpaper or contact paper. If you're really clever, put wheels on the boxes, or tie the

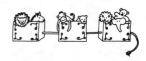

boxes together with string! But either way, fun is in store for your preschoolers as they give their favorite animals a ride.

Fabric Art

Have on hand an old white sheet and some color markers. As each child arrives, let her draw a favorite circus animal on the sheet. You may want to add the children's names to their artwork, or have them do it if they can. Save the sheet as a reminder of the party. It also can be covered with clear plastic and used as a tablecloth.

A Miniature Circus

Rope off circus rings in the yard with rope, string, the garden hose, or whatever you can find. Each ring can be a performance area for costumed guests. One ring could feature singers; another, acrobats or dancers; another, jugglers. A happy music cassette adds to the atmosphere. After the performance, serve clown cupcakes, cookies, and juice.

A Circus Parade

Let each child choose an animal to be and select a ringmaster to lead the "animals." You could organize the parade in your "circus ring" and conduct the parade like reverse musical chairs. Mark a spot in the ring. As the "animals" parade, the ringmaster could blow a whistle. Whoever is on the marked spot changes places with the ringmaster.

You can have a celebration for no reason at all. Help your family today to appreciate the good things and those worthy of our joy.

Surprise Favors

Collect cardboard rolls from toilet paper long before you start this one! Fill each tube with wrapped hard candy. Place the roll on a large sheet of colored tissue paper, colored cellophane, or gift wrap. Bring the wrap upwards; tie off the extra wrap with ribbon or yarn. Keep one end of the ribbon long. Cut a small name tag from colored construction paper, punch a hole in one end of it, and tie it on with the long ribbon.

Birthday Traditions

Many family traditions cluster around birthdays and Christmas. In the Dillow family the birthday person plans the menu for the entire day. So on Mom's and Dad's birthdays the meals are expensive and elegant. And on the children's birthdays the meals are—you guessed it— *junky!* For example, on Tommy's birthday he chose pancakes for breakfast; pizza for lunch; hamburgers, French fries, and milk shakes for dinner. But what fun Tommy had planning his own special meals!

A friend shared this birthday tradition: "Our most important gift to our birthday child is prayer because it is an investment in his life in eternity. On the birthday morning, my husband and I rise an hour earlier than usual to pray specifically for the child. We pray for his future, his mate, his education, his friends, his growth in Christ, and his character. We also read together passages of Scripture. That hour passes very quickly, and the day begins with a bubble of joy in our hearts."

Snow Party in a Box

You can pack your snow boxes in advance! When it snows, you'll be ready. Who cares if there's no school? So what if you can't get your car out of the driveway? The snow box will be ready, and the fun can begin.

The wonders of a snow box are the simple pleasures it holds. You fill your snow box with everything you need for a snow party. The basics for a sample snow party are

- 6 cans of Beanie Weenies™ (or any canned lunch quickies)
- 1 canister of hot chocolate mix
- 1 bag of marshmallows
- 2 cans of chili beans
- 1 package of mild chili seasoning mix
- 4 cans of tomato sauce
- 1 box of Rice Krispies™
- 1 small jar of peanut butter
- 1 small bottle of corn syrup
- 1 Ziploc™ bag (or margarine tub) with at least 1 c. sugar in it
- 1 pair of gloves per child and adult
- 1 hat per child and adult
- 1 pair of snow boots or plastic shoe covers per child and adult
- 1 craft kit

The only things you need for a great snow day that can't be put in the snow box are one pound of ground beef or turkey and a festive mood. (The ground meat should be frozen and hidden way in the back of the freezer so that no one will find it.) Put it under the turkey slices you froze after Thanksgiving, the ones you were going to use in a casserole some day.

The canned beans and wieners are for lunch. Feel free to substitute your own favorite canned lunch. The requirements are that it be quick, easy, storable, and cheap enough to share with snow party friends. If you have a wood stove, you might want to warm the food on top of it.

After lunch, when everyone needs a break from the snow play and you need time for the gloves to dry, bring out the simple craft kit. Consider the following:

- A bag of different colors of yarn and ribbon to make into friendship bracelets
- A bag of ribbons for making hair bows
- An air-dry pottery clay kit
- Ingredients to make play dough (see pages 52–53 for recipes).

A VIP Party

H ow better to help one child like a very important person than by letting her feel like "queen for a day!" King for a day if he's a boy.

One family chose to have a party in honor of their oldest son when he began his first summer job picking strawberries. Hot, bone weary, and aching from head to toe, he stumbled into the house one evening to discover posters, presents, and poems—all with his name on them. It was a party to express his family's love and to show him that they were on his team.

The walls were decorated with posters that said, "My brother is great! He wins the Strawberry Picker Award!" "We love Ryan." Silly gifts had been wrapped and were stacked at his place at the table. With each gift was a poem or note to express appreciation. The meal was his favorite; the dessert, extra special.

After dinner each family member gave Ryan a coupon saying what they would do for him the following week: "I will empty the trash for you." "I will make your bed for one week." After dinner a slide show was given in his honor, showing pictures of his life from the first year to the present. He was the "star" for one night.

Think for a moment about how you would feel if your family spent the time to plan a VIP Party in your honor. That is exactly how each of your children or your husband would feel.

Use a day to plan a VIP Party for another family member, a special friend, or an elderly neighbor. The day can be spent together cooking the food, making "we love you" posters, drawing pictures, wrapping silly gifts, preparing a slide show and letting the children write a script, practicing a song to sing, thinking of special things to do the following week as coupon gifts. Let your imagination run wild, or better yet, ask your children (their imaginations are *already* wild) what they would like to do for the special person.

Or you might plan a VIP Party for one child while she is visiting relatives or friends or is away at camp and the other children are at home with you. What fun it is to plan a special surprise party for the brother or sister who is gone!

Sometimes VIP Parties are in order even when they are quite inconvenient for you . . .

- . . . when Dad worked hard on a project at work for months and he just called to say it has all fallen through
- . . . when the neighborhood kids laughed at your child because of her new braces and she says she's not smiling for two years
- . . . when your child has studied hard for his exam but studied the wrong things
- . . . when a super summer week has been planned and your child comes down with chicken pox
- . . . when Mom "gracefully" trips over the sidewalk curb and breaks her ankle. She *needs* a party!

Remember to pick and choose from these activities. Don't try to do everything if that leaves you feeling overwhelmed.

*O*ther Fun Ideas for Celebrating a VIP

S ee Dave and Claudia Arp's *60 One-Minute Memory Builders*—Part One, "You Are Special." If you are a single and/or working parent, these ideas will help you find the time to let your child know he is special.

A Half Birthday

H ave a half cake and a half present. Sing half of "Happy Birthday." Invite half as many people, but have twice as much fun! This idea is especially good for children who have a birthday around Christmas or in the summer when their friends are on vacation.

A Spiritual Birthday

When your child becomes a Christian, you can help her to write out her experience or tape it and gather family and friends to share in it.

A Back-to-School Party

Use lunch boxes as serving dishes. Let each child dress in the clothing to be worn on the first day of school. Make a list as a family of what each child is looking forward to that year; save this list for a Last-Day-of-School Party in the spring. Then make a list of things to pray about for each child for the coming school year, and pray together.

A Babysitter Appreciation Party

Invite your favorite babysitter over for a VIP Party. Write a poem about the sitter's best sitting skills. Make a little gift, and serve punch and cookies or cake and ice cream.

*M*om and Dad's Anniversary

O lder kids can cook the meal, something easy from Chapter 10. They can set an elegant table, and direct dinner conversation to stories of how Mom and Dad met and decided to get married. The kids can also videotape or tape record these stories.

A Party for "100"

I s it the 100th day of the year? The 100th day of school? Did a child get a well-deserved 100 on a test? You pick the occasion and enjoy a 100 Day with your children. Try these ideas with your young ones.

Put 100 pennies in rice! The children will get more and more excited as they dig through the rice for the disappearing coins. Then have them divide the pennies into groups of 10. Math skills and fun too!

Give your children small containers and ask them to find 100 small things. Then name each thing and tell what its function is. For example, your child may put a paperclip into her box; she must name it and explain what it does.

Make a book with this theme: "My mom has told me 100 times . . ." Make sure to keep this for lots of laughs in later years!

If a man insisted always on being serious, and never allowed himself a bit of fun and relaxation, he would go mad or become unstable without knowing it.

Herodotus
The Histories of Herodotus, Book II

CHAPTER 14

Special Kids, Special Times

*S*ince we have little experience in developing appropriate activities for a special needs child, we learned from the experts. Julia Francis Clark, an occupational therapist at the East Tennessee Children's Rehabilitation Center in Knoxville, Tennessee, provided us with several ideas for general use. Above all, she says, "Praise, praise, praise your child, not for performance or results, but for *effort!*" Leigh Krieps, employed by the Therapy Center in Knoxville, Tennessee, also sent ideas.

*D*eveloping Skills While Having Fun

Practice Mouth Posturing

Encourage your child to imagine situations and make appropriate mouth responses. You can help by offering effective audible cues like, "A fly's going to fly into your mouth! Here comes a fly!" Be positive and light as you offer these cues. You might lightly tap the lower lip to focus the child's attention there.

You can also make a kiss noise to remind your child to close his mouth.

String Beads

To strengthen fine motor skills, string beads, beginning with large ones and progressing to smaller ones. Your child can even wear the resulting necklace or bracelet! Or he can make one for Mom or a sister or friend.

Play Thumbs-Up with Scissors

Scissors with two different colored blades often help children to remember which is the thumb side. Or help with a repetitive cue like "Thumbs go in the blue part (or "upper part") of the handle." "Thumbs up!" is a good cue for both scissor hand and paper hand.

Play Dress-Up

Playing dress-up in Mom's or Dad's old clothes is a great way to improve frustration tolerance. Have the child put on an old shirt and play "button up like Mommy/Daddy." Alternate buttons and turns, buttoning one and then the next button.

Work Puzzles with a Timer

A jigsaw puzzle can be used to prolong your child's attention span. Buy a puzzle appropriate for your child's tolerance. Or make your own from a family picture or magazine picture (see directions on page 62). Set the kitchen timer, building gradually up from one minute to four minutes. Give these instructions: "Work the best you can until you hear the buzzer!"

You can also use this idea with drawing: "I will draw with you for three minutes, until we hear the buzzer."

Take an Animal Walk

The plan is simple: Once every night, walk from one room to another (twenty feet or more—say, from dinner table to bedroom) doing any animal walk. Go slowly if form is poor. Here are some fun suggestions:

A Alligator
B Bear

N (g)Nat (flap arms for wings)

C Crab (backward on all fours)

D Duck (squat walk)

E Elephant

F Frog

G Giraffe (tiptoes)

H Horse (gallop)

I Inchworm (arms walk out, legs catch up)

J Jaguar

K Kangaroo

L Lion

M Monkey

O Octopus (sit straddled, slide backward)

P Pig

Q Queen Bee

R Rabbit

S Snake (no arms)

T Tarantula (hands walk, feet jump)

U Unicorn (gallop with a horn)

V Viper

W Walrus (straight arms, drag legs)

Z Zebra (gallop)

It could be fun—and good exercise—to do this activity with your child. Or you might invite the whole family to join in.

Games to Improve Fine Motor-Eye/ Hand Coordination and Motor Planning

Lifting a Finger

Place your hand flat on a table or on the floor. Lift one finger at a time while keeping the others still. Do this thirty times with each finger. (The ring finger may need extra help!) When you become comfortable with this exercise, try two hands at the same time.

Fingertip Isometrics

Place a rubber band snugly over two fingers at a time close to the fingertips. If the band is large, double or triple twist it until it is fairly snug. Separate the enclosed fingers, thirty times for each pair.

Row, Row, Row Your Boat

Hold your forearm still (someone else can help if needed), and rotate a pencil or a stick on either side of your hand—as if you were rowing a boat. The bathtub is a great place for this activity. Keep your forearm level with and a few inches above the water surface.

You could also use a two-ended pencil held a few inches above a piece of paper.

Wiggler

Spend one minute wiggling a pencil between two neighboring fingers.

Twirler

Pinch a pencil between the thumb and pointer finger. Then move it to between your small and ring fingers by twirling. Use only one hand at a time!

Tricky Twirler

If you want to be extra tricky, try twirling your pencil from between your pointer and middle fingers to between your pinky and ring fingers.

Catch!

To improve bilateral coordination and motor planning skills, well, of all things, play catch! The whole family will want to take part in this activity. Throw various-sized balls in different ways:

Take time to know your children. You'll be the winner, and your kids will be your friends for life!

- Backward, through legs
- Under one leg
- Around your back
- Over your head
- Underhanded
- With one hand or with two

Strong Arm Play

Short Ride

Ask your child to sit on a skateboard or scooter and hold on to a rope that has been fastened to a stationary object. Then pull the skateboard or scooter. The stronger the child's arms, the shorter the ride.

Push/Pull

Two people hold on to a large ball and play push/pull. Match your child's abilities while encouraging the child's strength and effort.

Bean Bag Toss

Make bean bags of varied weights out of baggies and dried beans (available at any grocery). Have the child toss the bean bags into a bucket. This game also helps to improve eye-hand coordination.

Tilt-a-Kid

Have your child sit on your lap and tilt from side to side and backward; encourage her to return to midline (belly-button-middle) each time.

Creative Clay Play

Playing with play dough or modeling clay (see recipes for homemade play dough pp. 52–53) will help your child to strengthen hand muscles. Rave over the inventions, have a showing at the dinner table, and have fun!

Finger Painting

Encourage your child to color or finger paint in solutions such as paint or pudding. Make lines up, down, across and in circles, intentionally naming each motion: "I'm going up . . . down . . . round and round." Move your child's hand through these motions as you say the words.

Practice these same strokes in the dirt when you are outdoors with your child. Use your finger, a stick, or a pencil.

This art project also helps to improve eye-hand coordination.

Fun Ways to Improve Eye/ Hand Coordination

Popping Bubbles

Blow soap bubbles for your child and have him pop them between his hands. Set a reasonable goal, and cheer your child on as he approaches it.

Architect

Encourage your child to stack blocks one atop the other to make towers.

Ball Play!

Roll a medium-sized ball to your child and have her roll it back to you.

Ring Placement

Encourage him to place large plastic rings over a stand.

Balloon Volley

Inflate a balloon and toss it in the air. Ask the child to hit the balloon as many times as she can before it hits the floor or the ground.

Big League Player

Inflate a balloon and tie it with a string. Hang the balloon from the ceiling or doorway, and let the child "bat" the balloon with a yardstick or any other smooth stick that is long enough. He can pretend to be his favorite baseball star.

Turn this into a tennis game and let her "be" a favorite tennis star when you have her hit the ball using only one arm at a time.

Flashlight Tag

This one is good for after-dark play. Dim the lights in a room, or play outside. Flash a flashlight beam at various points around the area. Ask the child to "tag" the area with a hand or foot. (Note: Flash quickly from one spot to the next.)

Milk Jug Bowling

Set up plastic half-gallon milk jugs like bowling pins. Roll an orange, a grapefruit, or a ball to knock down the jugs. Try ten times, and keep a score of the jugs knocked down.

Modified Seven-Up

The child stands approximately four feet from the wall, inside or outside, and throws the ball against the wall and tries to catch it as it bounces back. Give one point for each good try, two points for each ball caught.

ABC Toss

This game is to be played outside. Have your child throw a ball straight up as far as he can and begin reciting the ABCs until the ball hits the ground. The object is to throw the ball higher each time and to get farther through the ABCs.

Moving Ball Toss

You'll need a medium to large box, a ball (or an orange or grapefruit). Have your child throw the ball into the box. After each successful throw, move the box to another place in each room. Provide a new challenge with each move.

Improving Arm and Upper Body Strength

Hanging Out

Go to a nearby playground and literally "hang out!" Climb, hang, pull, and push. Swinging is a good way to combine all these exercises.

Tug-O-War

Place a flag in the middle of a rope. You take one end of the rope and have the child take the other. The object is to pull until you touch the flag. Let your child win, but not always, and certainly put up a good enough fight to challenge your child's strength! This game can be made more difficult if it is played in a tall kneeling position.

Wheelbarrow Walking

Do you remember seeing or participating in partner wheelbarrow races at the fair? Try it! Hold your child's feet while she "walks" forward with her hands. The body stays generally straight.

Bear Walking

To do a bear walk, crawl on hands and feet rather than hands and knees.

Pre-Writing and Scissor Exercise

Cutout Play Dough Cookies

To help your child gain confidence and practice with scissors, let him cut flattened play dough. Imprint a design in clay or play dough and have her cut it out.

Fancy Paper Cutting

If you want your child to cut paper, stiff paper (like construction paper) and index cards are much easier to cut than regular paper, and much more rewarding and motivating to the new cutter.

Remind your child to stabilize the paper with the non-preferred hand, or provide her with a clipboard!

Finger Writing

Let your child practice scribbling strokes and directionality in shaving cream, finger paints, etc. Show the child how to use his hands, just his fingers, and alternate fingers one at a time.

Stencil Play

Buy or make simple stencils, and then let your child play with them. When she becomes comfortable with them, have her close her eyes and trace them with her fingers.

Racetrack

Make a "racetrack in the sand," using any pre-writing shape (a figure 8, for instance). Encourage your child to follow the path with a toy car.

Star Tracking

Place gummed stars at the beginning, end, and corners of shapes. Have the child draw from star to star! Let him know what a fine star tracker you think he is!

Squares and Circles

When drawing or cutting shapes, be creative. Instead of squares, squares, squares, think about televisions, cereal boxes, books, pictures, lunch boxes. Circles could be balloons, balls, bubbles, door knobs, tires. . . .

Shape Tracing

Try tracing shapes with a finger first, then with a marker, then with a crayon or pencil. And you don't need to restrict yourself to paper for finger tracing. You can "draw" in sand, shaving cream, or salt.

Activity Book Choices

Help your child to follow a maze or play dot-to-dot.

Letter Construction

Cut vinyl into small-scale letter pieces suitable for table-top use. The pattern is below. One mom cut the pieces out of a plain red placemat. The vinyl is about ⅛″ thick and is easy to cut. Your child can prepare for learning to print by constructing letters from these pieces. A Head Start teacher learned how this system works and said, "Well, that's worth cutting up a placemat."

How much you will rely on these pieces depends on your child's needs. They are particularly helpful for young children or for children with perceptual-motor problems. To give your child enough to make any letter, allow 4 big lines, 3 little lines, 2 big curves, and 2 little curves.

Constructing a letter before attempting to write it greatly facilitates writing. You can easily help your child to solve any problems with size, shape, or placement by moving these pieces. His ability and confidence are strengthened each time he has selected and placed each piece in the correct sequence.

Try this method: You construct a letter out of pieces,

and ask your child to imitate you piece by piece. Then print the letter on plain paper. Ask your child to imitate each step in printing the letter.

Your verbal instructions might go like this: "Watch me write an *H*. I start at the top beside the smiley face. I write a big line down. Now it is your turn. . . . I am going to write another big line down. Now you do it. . . . Now I'll write a little line across the middle. Your turn . . . That's an *H!* You made and *H*—good for you."

*B*alancing Activities

Hopping and Jumping

Make the most of your child's energy! Play hopscotch! Jump rope! Learn some of the current rhymes and rhythms children use as they jump rope. Draw numbers or figures on the driveway or sidewalk or tape a figure on the floor, and do the bunny hop along the lines. Put on some fun music, or let your child sing a favorite song until she's done.

Stepping Stones

Stepping stones are helpful for balance, and they needn't be just gardening stones! Place large blocks a suitable distance apart, and have your child walk or hop from one to the next. Use one foot or two.

Perfect Pointer

Have your child get down on all fours, then balance on three body parts, then two, then one. Then he can lift the opposite arm and leg straight out and bark like a dog—a perfect pointer!

Every Which Way

Have your child walk forward, backward, and sideways on a crooked taped line. Go slowly.

Curb Walking

Your child can walk along a curb, keeping balance with one foot on the curb, the other on the street.

Calling for . . . .

Have the child balance on one leg, close her eyes, and name five ice cream flavors. Then she can switch legs and try again, this time naming pizza toppings. And so on.

Balancing on a Ball

Ask your child to lie on a big ball, face down, then lift opposite arm and leg and count "One, two, three." Then reverse arm and leg.

A variation on this balancing act is to lift arms only or legs only.

Heel and Toe

In this fun exercise the child walks the length of the room on his heels—whistling; then he walks back on his toes—humming.

Child of the pure, unclouded brow
And dreaming eyes of wonder!
Though time be fleet and I and thou
Are half a life asunder,
Thy loving smile will surely hail
The love-gift of a fairy tale.

Lewis Carroll
Through the Looking-Glass

Tape Hopping

Place pieces of tape on the floor about eight inches apart all over the room. Your child can then hop on one leg, stopping to balance for three seconds on each piece of tape. After she has landed on all pieces of tape, she can shift to the other leg and hop back through the room.

Sit-Down Time

Place assorted chairs, stools, and pillows around the room. Your child can then slowly sit down on each seat without using his hands.

Balance Beam

Make a "balance beam" of an outside low wall, curb, sidewalk, or edging. Have your child extend her arms out, walk along the "beam." She can pretend that she's in the Olympics.

General Strength-Building Activities

Head and Toe

Your child lies on his back. You place a ball between his feet. He raises the ball with his feet, raises his head at the same time, and holds that position until he can name five colors (kinds of cookies, kinds of animals, etc.).

Backup

Have your child back up to a wall. Place a medium to large ball between the wall and the child's back. Ask your child to hold the ball against the wall and slowly bend her knees, rolling the ball down, then straighten back up again—without dropping the ball. Repeat this one ten times.

Knee Ball

While your child is sitting, place a ball between his knees. He squeezes the ball in with his knees and holds the position until he names five games (animals, neighbors, etc.). Repeat ten times.

Vary this one by asking the child to hold a small ball in his hand, squeezing it while he names five types of juice, etc. Repeat ten times.

Tiptoe Balance

The child faces a wall, placing her hands on the wall for balance. She rises up on her toes and names five cartoon characters, etc. Repeat ten times.

Leg Lifts

The child lies on his side and lifts the top leg up and down slowly, counting backward from twenty. Repeat on the other side.

Touch-the-Dot

Place a dot or circle on a wall. Your child can stand facing the wall with arms extended, hands touching the wall. Then she bends her arms, letting her body come in until her nose touches the dot. Then she pushes back out. Repeat ten times.

General Coordination

Foot Catch

While your child sits on the floor, roll a ball toward her. She must catch the ball with her feet only.

Obstacle Course

Set up chairs, boxes, pillows, baskets. Your child hops over, crawls around, and crawls under various objects. He can pretend he's in Marine training.

Follow the Leader

In this outside game, hop on one foot, clap hands overhead, run, walk very slowly, walk backward, raise arms up and down, etc. Anyone who wants can join in the fun.

Back in the Box

Place various objects (fruit, soup cans, toys, shoes, etc.) around a large area indoors or out. Place a big box beside the child as a starting point. Your child runs, picks up an object, brings it back to the box. Set a timer for one minute and encourage him to get as many objects into the box as possible in that time.

CHAPTER 15

Just You and Me Times

*A*s parents, our greatest challenge is to love our children in a healthy, full, God-honoring way. One way to do this is to spend time with them—quiet, personal, together time.

Times for Two are focused times you spend alone with one child. A Time for Two can be as simple as ten minutes of finger play with a toddler on the floor or a planned afternoon outing with your ten-year-old. Younger children love it when you talk about and have Times for Two. Older children still need the focused time together, but smart parents don't call it that! Throughout this book, you'll find other activities and suggestions for Times for Two.

*T*ime for Two Coupon Book

T o ensure that you actually do spend frequent one-to-one time with your children, give each child a Time for Two Coupon Book.

Materials needed:

- Index cards
- Cute stickers
- Yarn or ribbon
- Hole puncher
- Felt markers

Punch two holes on one end of the cards. Decorate the cards with stickers. Write out coupons for each child, using one card for one coupon. Tie each child's coupons together with yarn.

Give coupons to the child. Together with the child, schedule times for each coupon.

Suggested coupons:

- Cooking with parent
- Reading with parent
- Shopping with Dad or Mom
- Playing a favorite game with Mom or Dad
- Putting together a simple puzzle with Dad or Mom
- A hot chocolate date with Mom or Dad

*R*eading for Enjoyment

T his coupon could provide many special Times for Two as you and your child travel with the little Pilgrim in *Little Pilgrim's Progress*. Not only will both of you enjoy the book, but it will open the door to many wonderful discussions.

We have found some excellent "read-aloud" books.

Preschoolers

- Arch Books—short books in poem form that teach biblical truths (Concordia)
- *Winnie the Pooh* or *The House at Pooh Corner* by A. A. Milne (Dutton)
- *Make Way for Ducklings* by Robert McClosky (Viking)
- *Curious George* by Margaret and H. A. Rays (Houghton-Mifflin)
- *Little Visits with God* by Jahsmann and H. A. Rays (Houghton-Mifflin)

A preschooler needs to have a book finished in one session, so perhaps you might pick several books to read aloud over a few weeks. Little tots love lots of pictures! You might make a special reading coupon and include a visit to the library so that the child can help select the books.

School-Age Children

- *Little Pilgrim's Progress* by Helen L. Taylor (Moody)
- *Little House on the Prairie* series by Laura Ingalls Wilder (Harper)
- *Chronicles of Narnia* series by C. S. Lewis (Macmillan)
- *Treasure of the Snow* and *Lost on the Trail* by Patricia St. John (Moody)
- *The Boxcar Children* series by Gertrude Chandler Warner (Alber Whitman & Co.)
- *Mrs. Piggle-Wiggle* series by Betty MacDonald (Lippincott)

Finding Open Gates

Watch for times your child appears to be open. Be ready with impromptu activities such as

- A cookie break—Don't just bake cookies. Sit down and eat them together
- A game of Double Solitaire
- Listening to music or watching a TV program of his choice
- Making a collage of items from your kitchen—cereal, macaroni, noodles, beans

Finger Puppets

Materials needed:

- Old gloves—rubber or fabric (or sacrifice a new rubber glove for the cause of communication)
- Felt-tip pen

Cut one finger of an old glove. Decorate with a felt-tip pen. Place over your finger and wiggle.

Sock Puppets

M aterials needed:

- Old socks (If your washing machine "eats" socks like ours does, you should have several "solo" socks.)
- Fabric and yarn scraps
- Buttons and other trims
- Glue or glue stick
- Felt-tip pens
- Scissors
- Needle and thread

Put socks over hand. Glue or sew button eyes where your fist fits into the sock. Add a felt tongue or ears or a hat, or draw the face with felt pens. If you want, you can create a whole "family" of puppets.

Box Puppets

M aterials needed:

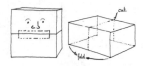

- Small individual cereal boxes (the kind that are supposed to keep kids from fighting over cereal)
- Paper and yarn scraps
- Crayons or felt-tip pens
- Scissors
- Glue or glue stick
- Knife

Do not open cereal box by tearing off end. An adult opens it by cutting with a sharp knife across the center and down both sides. Fold on remaining fourth side (see sketch). Decorate with scraps and crayons. Insert hand and move fingers to make puppet talk.

Sack Puppets

Materials needed:

- Lunch-size paper bag
- Scraps of fabric, paper, yarn, felt
- Glue
- Scissors
- Crayons, felt-tip pens, or paints

Glue or draw a face on the bottom of a bag. The fold in the bag is used for the mouth opening. Add yarn for hair and whiskers. You may want to add a paper hat or ears. Let your child create!

Time for Two Cookie Bake

Let your child choose a favorite recipe. Bake the cookies or make the candy alone with one child! Here's a simple cookie recipe:

Mix thoroughly:

⅓ c. soft shortening	*⅔ c. honey*
⅓ c. sugar	*1 t. vanilla*
1 egg	

Stir in:

> *2¾ c. sifted flour*
> *1 t. soda*
> *1 t. salt*

Chill the cookie dough. Heat the oven to 375°. Roll the dough out to ¼" thickness. Cut it in different shapes. Bake 8 to 10 minutes on a greased baking sheet. Makes five dozen 2½" cookies.

This is a great recipe for making Paintbrush Cookies (see page 209), a fun project for the two of you.

We-Two-Fixed-It Dinner

T̲ogether plan a simple menu, and let your child help with the preparation. A fun cookbook for parent and child is *Kids Cooking—A Very Slightly Mess Manual* (Klutz Press, 1987). You can order this book from Klutz Press, 2121 Staunton Court, Palo Alto, California 94306.

On a cold winter day, you might want to try soup. If you are really industrious, plan a soup buffet. Use three or four different soup mixes and let your family pick and choose. Serve soup with a loaf of homemade bread. You can purchase loaves of dough from the frozen food section of the grocery. All you have to do is let it thaw and rise and then bake it. To make the crust thick and crunchy, spray it with water a couple of times while the bread is baking.

If you like starting from scratch, consider making this easy soup recipe.

Start today and use the little moments you do have to build memories. When your children grow up and leave home, they won't leave empty-handed.

Easy Vegetable Soup

1 lb. lean ground beef	1 10-oz. bag frozen
1 envelope onion soup	peas
mix	1 10-oz. bag frozen
2 stalks celery	green beans
½ c. barley	1 10-oz. bag frozen
1 46-oz. can vegetable	corn
juice	8 c. water

Cook ground beef until it crumbles. Drain fat; then put meat in a colander and rinse with hot water to remove any extra fat. Place all the ingredients in a 5-qt. Dutch oven. Simmer until the barley is done. Makes 4 quarts.

Here's another quick recipe:

Very Quick Spaghetti

¼ c. oil	Bay leaf
2 cans tomato paste	Oregano
1 46-oz. can tomato	Tabasco
juice	Salt and pepper to
3 T. sugar	taste

Over medium heat in a heavy pot, add oil to cover the bottom of the pan and prevent the tomato paste from sticking. Add tomato paste and then stir in the tomato juice. Add the sugar; then add the seasonings—any/all/some/little, depending on how spicy you want the sauce. Simmer over low heat up to one hour.

OPTIONAL: Brown lean ground beef in the pot before you add the tomato paste. Or sauté chopped onions in the oil until golden; then add paste.

Photo Place Cards

For table decorations, make place cards with baby pictures of each family member. Each must find his own picture.

Another recipe for a Time for Two right before dinner allows chat time during peeling, stirring, and "dropping."

Apple Drop Biscuits

Preheat the oven to 450°.

½ c. apple juice	1 small apple, peeled
2 c. Bisquick	½ t. cinnamon
2 T sugar	¼ t. nutmeg

Shred the apple. Combine Bisquick, sugar, cinnamon, and nutmeg. Pour the apple juice into a bowl; add the Bisquick mixture and shredded apples. Stir with a wooden spoon until wet. The batter should be lumpy, so don't stir it too much.

Grease a cookie sheet. Drop the mixture by tablespoons onto the cookie sheet. Bake 10 to 12 minutes.

These are especially good with honey butter.

CHAPTER 16

Fun to Fill the Gap
(or Long-Distance Bridge Builders)

*W*hat a pleasure to be able to sit across the table from your little loves! There's nothing like personal contact! So what happens when your precious ones are far and wide? We creatively love them *long distance!*

Building relationships by long distance is a challenge faced by many in our mobile society. We both have spent many years living in Europe and offer here creative possibilities to help span the miles and deepen the relationships, even when an ocean or many miles separate you from those you love.

Here you will find some ideas for building relationships long distance.

Send a Cookie

You can make your displaced family member feel right at home with a carefully packaged batch of cookies and a cheerful note. Or if the absent one has a place for baking try sending a cookie dough mix. You'll find the recipe in Chapter 10.

Telephone Privileges

If the family is separated over a long period of time, a family 800 number can provide ready access to parents, grandparents, children. Call your long distance telephone service to find out whether this is something that your family would like to do.

A Bookful of Love

H ere is an idea for grandparents to do with their grand-children. They can buy each grandchild an inexpensive copy book and put in pictures and photos of things that will interest the grandchild, from magazines, greeting cards, postcards, and the like. They'll want to leave plenty of blank pages too. After they give the book to the grand-children, they can write weekly and send new pictures for the book. The grandchildren will love getting mail and putting the pictures in their own granparents' book. Even if they see their grandparents only twice a year, the grand-children will never forget the family members who send them such pleasures.

A Tape for Grandmother/father

S end a tape or video to a grandparent and encourage Grandma or Grandpa to send one back. The children can sing, tell stories about their daily lives, and ask the latest third-grade riddle on the tape or video they send. Then the grandparent can read stories to the children on the tape, and the children can listen to it as they go to sleep. This will keep them in touch with far-away family.

A Story Tape for Friends or Family

A most creative gift for loved ones far away is a "secret" story tape. The only materials you will need are a pen, blank paper (some aged-looking paper for a special effect), a blank tape, and the inexpensive gifts that your imaginations suggest. Start with an explanatory note:

Dear Friends.

Open only when you are alone as a family and have at least an hour to spare!

> Love,
> Clark and Ann

Put a story on an "old" parchment. Your family can create a story. (Or you may use the one below, modifying the family details to fit the family to whom you send it.) Together discuss each child in the chosen family and pick out one special thing about her personality that you could weave into a story. For example, you might remember that the youngest daughter is athletic and plays soccer. Get your story going and then leave it unfinished for the receiving family to continue.

Your gifts can be little things you have around the house and can weave into the story—pencils, rocks, toy boats, planes, cars. You can use *anything!*

A SECRET SEVEN STORY FOR YOU TO FINISH

Once upon a time in the land of Walwyth (pronounced wall-with), there was a very great and good king who had a lovely wife as queen and three handsome sons. The king and his wife helped many people. One time when they returned from a long trip, they brought each son a gift.

To the eldest son, they gave a jeweled knife; to the middle son, they gave a knife with a seahorse; and to the youngest son, they gave a many-colored glass. (The secret of these gifts was that each contained special powers because it was given in love by friends who cared!)

There was peace in the land where the young princes lived, but in the neighboring lands there was war. Sometimes bad men sneaked into Walwyth and did evil deeds. Usually these raiders were caught and punished by the king's guards, but one afternoon when the princes were out riding their ponies and practicing with their bows and arrows, something unexpected happened.

The king had sent all his soldiers away on an urgent mission, and some raiders disguised as palace guards rode right into the castle courtyard, robbed the king's treasure chest, and kidnapped the king and queen!

When the princes returned, they heard loud crying. Soon they learned what had happened and discovered there was no one to pursue the robbers and rescue the king and queen.

The youngest son said, "We must go after them at once!"

The second son said, "Yes, but first we should quickly pack a lunch and make ready because we don't know how long it will take to rescue them!"

The oldest son, with a serious expression on his face, gave the order for all to be made ready. He had the ponies fed and a pack horse brought to carry the tent, extra supplies, and food for the princes' dogs, who always went with them.

When all was ready, the princes knelt in a circle and asked God for wisdom and protection. Then they mounted their ponies and at a full gallop rode in the direction the kidnappers had gone. Each had tucked his magic gift safely in a pocket.

The tracks of the raiders were clear, and the princes followed them steadily toward the coast of Mania. There must have been about twenty in the raiding party, and one was probably a giant! His horse's tracks were as big

*as a dinner plate and sank deep into the ground because
of the weight. Other tracks showed that wild dogs ran
alongside the raiders' horses.*

*How were they going to rescue their parents and get
the treasure back?*

We'd love to hear the end you give this adventure!

Love,
Clark and Ann

Along with the unfinished story, wrap and send your
special gift for each child, the gift identified in the story.
Also send a blank tape for the family to record "the rest
of the story." Send the package off at your local post office,
and return home for juice, cookies, and lots of fun specu-
lating about what your friends will say when they get
your special package!

Your story will provide at least an hour of fun for the
receiving family as they fantasize their own personalized
fairy tale. If you have woven the family's personalities
into the story, you will be delighted when you hear the
finished expression of those personalities on the tape the
family makes and sends back to you.

> The great man is
> he who does not
> lose his child's
> heart.
>
> Mencius
> *Works,* IV

A Closeness Art Project

S end an absent relative a picture, collage, or any other
work of art from each of your children. You can have
the children make a greeting card to go along with the
artwork. What a special gift for an older sibling at college
or a grandparent who wonders what the "grands" are
doing now!

CHAPTER 17

Best Fun from PEP Groups for Moms

*O*ver the years Moms have given us their best quick tips. Here is a collection of almost fifty favorites!

Mothers in our PEP (Parents Encouraging Parents) groups have different ages of children from babies to teenagers. One comment we often hear is "I wish I had joined PEP when my children were younger." But the encouraging message for them and for you, too, is that you can begin at any age to work on improving relationships.

Regardless of our children's ages or the date on the calendar, we can begin afresh to relate, love, nurture, and facilitate our children's lives.

PEP Groups for Moms is a small-group, video-based church resource to help moms build positive relationships with their children and also with other moms who have children the same age. For more information on how to start your own group, write to

PEP Groups for Moms
P.O. Box 90303
Knoxville, Tennessee 37990

- Make a birdfeeder by taking a pine cone and tying a string on one end. Spread peanut butter on it and sprinkle it with bird seed. Tie it onto a nearby tree.

- Write a book together. Each person takes a turn writing a page to continue the story.

- Letting your children help, add food coloring to everyday meals. Examples: scrambled eggs, pancakes.

- Play "store." Make play money from scrap paper, and line up things from the pantry for merchandise. Use the money to buy things, then bag them and pretend to carry them home. You can also save empty boxes of crackers, cookies, cereal, and so on, for the children to use as grocery items.

- Cut shapes out of potatoes and use them as stamps. Dip them in paint and make designs on paper.

- A great way to save money on wrapping paper and greeting cards is to have your child make them. You can buy a big roll of butcher paper and have them put designs on it using markers, colored pencils, crayons, paint, or inexpensive rubber stamps. You could even try the potato stamps above. Others appreciate the originality.

- Let a child sit in "Daddy's chair at the table to have a cup of milk with her favorite buddy stuffed animal, who *also* has a cup and a bib.

- Rice Play: Spoon dry rice from various containers to others. You can also use tubs that allow water to flow through, and it usually makes an appealing sound. This activity is best done on the patio for easy cleanup.

- Save or find larger boxes for the child to make his own fort, house, slide, or whatever. One family saved a big box, which their one-and-a-half-year-old uses as a slide. Another child created a house with her box by drawing in windows with curtains and a mailbox. She used magazine pictures to decorate it with flowers.

- Go to your library and check out a book of simple science experiments. With a little thought and a concordance, you can usually find a Scripture verse or character quality that relates to your experiment. For example, the writer of Proverbs says that "Like vinegar on soda is one who sings songs to a sad heart." When you mix vinegar and baking soda, it bubbles and "boils"— giving a great illustration of how someone would feel when we say, "Cheer up—it's not so bad."

- Throw rocks into a nearby lake, pond, or stream! Little children love this. If your pond has ducks, save your moldy bread or last few pieces and add even more easy entertainment.

- Play sports with your children because it's important for them to see *both* parents active in sport, whether it's throwing a football, kicking a soccer ball, or pitching a baseball.

- Make puppets out of socks by taping on eyes, mouths, etc., out of construction paper. You can even make a dinosaur by attaching an egg carton to the sock with rubber bands!

- Using old frozen juice lids, play Concentration. Put stickers on one side of each lid. Be sure that you have two—and only two—of each sticker. Turn the lids over, sticker side down, and try to remember where each sticker and its match is.

- Find major construction work and watch it from a safe place! The children are fascinated by the big machines.

If there is anything that we wish to change in the child, we should first examine it and see whether it is not something that could better be changed in ourselves.

Carl Jung
The Integration of the Personality

- Make your own book covers by decorating brown grocery bags!

- Let the children play Doot-Doot with Daddy or Mommy! The parent gets on all fours and chases toddlers through the house, calling, "Doot doot!" It's similar to tag. When the parent catches the child, it's tickle time! Sometimes the parent can crawl ahead and hide. The children love to "find" the parent and run! There are lots of giggles in this one!

- Stronghold: A parent can put one child behind him or her and let the other child try to "get" the protected child. The parent is the *stronghold* and never lets the child be "gotten." It's rollicking good fun, full of close calls, and a good lesson of how our heavenly Father is our stronghold and protection.

- If you have a nine-month-old to two-year-old, save colored caps from milk jugs and an empty can with a plastic lid (shortening, drink mix, an empty diaper wipes box, etc. Cut a hole in the plastic top that is large enough for the caps to pass through. Decorate the can with Contact paper or stickers. This game is great for hand-eye coordination.

- Make a homemade piñata with a plastic bag or paper bag filled with candy or small toys. Your kids can choose the toys and help to stuff the bags with paper.

- Have a treasure hunt with pennies or M&Ms. Hide the goodies all over the house. The kids can eat the candy or save the pennies.

- Cut a hole in a cardboard box. Fill baggies with dried beans and have a bean bag toss! Three-year-olds love this!

- Here's a continuing project for a preschooler: Keep a looseleaf binder filled with paper. Write out the letters of the alphabet, one per page. Give your child one of those zillions of catalogs and have them cut out objects. This can take twenty minutes to an hour! Then or at another time, sit down with the child and the glue stick and help the child put the pictures under the appropriate letter.

- In margarine tubs, add food coloring to dye rice. Then draw a picture on a piece of paper. With a toothpick apply the glue to rice and make a mosaic.

- Let your child look through old photos or scrapbooks. Help him name all the faces and tell him why those people are in there.

- Keep a container of things to "lace" together with thick yarn or thread or thick shoelaces: cereal, noodles, buttons, spools.

- When it's not too cold out, get an old blanket and a flashlight for each child. Go out and pretend to camp, and look at the stars. Then let the children look for things around the yard with their flashlights.

- Keep a "paint with water" book handy. If you use Q-tips instead of paintbrushes, you can also keep it simple by just using food coloring and water! Your child can sit at the kitchen table and paint and still be able to see you.

- Buy an apron for your child so that when you cook he can pretend to cook with you. Give him bowls and beans and spoons and pots so he can be busy! You can ask him to cook you something—he'll love it.

- A two-year-old can play with play dough and cookie cutters for fifteen or twenty minutes without supervision.

- Two-year-olds will also enjoy standing on a kitchen chair and "scrubbing" plastic dishes in the sink using a long-handled scrub brush. A parent should be close by for this!

- Keep a roll of cut-out cookies in the freezer and a can of frosting on hand. You can defrost the cookies and have your children decorate them the way they want to. In the summer they can do this outside on a picnic table—for easy cleanup.

- Next time you have a treasure hunt, leave little messages with the hidden items.

- Let your children enjoy water play with the hose. Let them wash the car, wash their bikes, water the flowers.

- Read a story to the children, and then have them act it out. They can repeat their performance for the rest of the family later.

- Hide special toys that haven't been played with for a while, and have the children hunt for them.

- Buy simple puzzles appropriate for your child's age.

- Give your children a box of colored chalk and let them draw on the driveway. It will wash off with the next rain.

- In your free time, record books on cassettes. Let your children listen when they wish. This is great for errand time in the car. You can even help your children learn Spanish or another language—in the car.

- In the fall, have your children pick up leaves and make rubbings.

- Collect pine cones and other nature items and make animals with glue.

- Buy—or share with other families—lots of character-building cassette tapes and tape player for each child. Send them to their rooms for a quiet time during the day. This is good for them and good for you!

- Make milk carton blocks! Cut the tops off and force two ½ gallon cartons together. Kids love these.

- If your children are cooped up, put on a good "rhythm tape," give them tambourines, sticks, or anything that will bang (marching and clapping work too) and let them go!

- Send your children out to "paint" the house with a bucket of water tinted with food coloring!

• On a big piece of paper, draw a house frame. Tape it to a wall, and then give your children an old Sears-type catalog to fill up all the rooms with furniture, people, and goodies.

• Use old magazines and catalogs to make a collage of "things in God's world that are good for me" or "things I am thankful for." This develops cutting and pasting skills and keeps kids busy for quite a while. The kids also tend to get along just great while they're doing this.

• Enjoy these ideas from other moms. You'll find even more ideas in *60 One-Minute Family Builders* and *60 One-Minute Memory Makers* by Dave and Claudia Arp (Thomas Nelson, 1993).

CHAPTER 18

A Look Back

*L*ooking at family fun from the vantage point of the empty nest, we ask ourselves, "If we could put life in reverse, go back and do it all over again, what would we do differently?"

First, we're not sure we would have the energy! Second, we would probably just make different mistakes the second time around. This we do know: We'd try to enjoy the process a lot more. We would definitely have more family fun!

If we had it to do over again, we'd make more cookies and sit and eat cookies and drink lemonade with our children. We'd take more nature hikes together even if the weather was uncooperative and we didn't feel like it. We'd laugh more with our kids and at ourselves. We'd worry less about mud and snow tracked on our carpets.

Wherever you are in your parenting pilgrimage, now is the time to begin. Much sooner than you think, the day will come when there will be

- No dripping bathing suits and towels on the bathroom floors,
- No extra traffic of little feet on your freshly vacuumed carpets,
- No music blaring,
- No hectic days in the car,
- No slammed doors.

Family Fun will be a memory; creative projects a thing of the past. There will be no more opportunities

- To listen, laugh, and love with your own children,
- To lead them to new truths about God, love, and life,
- To teach the joy of giving ourselves to others.

No, those unique opportunities will be gone. Our homes will once again be in order. All will be quiet. Then, as you look at your tidy house, you might like to

- Trip over a toy fire truck,
- See the garage lights left burning once again,
- Plan one more Family Fun time,
- Enjoy one more Time for Two.

But it will be too late. Our job with the children God has entrusted especially to us will be done.

Now is all the time we have . . .

Today . . .

Tomorrow . . .

This year . . .

Now is the time for building the future. Now is the time to use *The Big Book of Family Fun!*

Resources from the Arps

Parents Encouraging Parents (PEP) Resources

- PEP Groups for MOMS Video Package by Claudia Arp contains a 5-part video series entitled, *Building Positive Relationships with Children,* a Director's Handbook, Leader's Guide, and individual study book for participants. Elgin, IL: David C. Cook Publishing Company, 1994.

Family Resources

- PEP Groups for Parents of Teens Video Package by Dave & Claudia Arp, contains a 5-part video series entitled *Building Positive Relationships for the Teen Years,* a Director's Handbook, Leader's Guide, and individual study books for participants. Elgin, Illinois: David C. Cook Publishing Company, 1994.

- *The Big Book of Family Fun* by Claudia Arp and Linda Dillow, contains year-round creative activities that the whole gang will love. Nashville: Thomas Nelson Publishers, 1994.

- *60 One-Minute Family Builders, 60 One-Minute Memory Makers,* and *60 One-Minute Marriage Builders* by Dave and Claudia Arp are three little books to help you use the time you do have to build your own family team. Nashville: Thomas Nelson Publishers, 1993.

- *52 Ways to Be a Great Mother-in-Law* by Claudia Arp, contains practical helps for keeping extended family relationships healthy. Nashville: Thomas Nelson Publishers, 1993.

Marriage Resources by Dave and Claudia Arp

- *The Ultimate Marriage Builder*—A do-it-yourself Encounter Weekend for you and your mate. Nashville: Thomas Nelson Publishers, 1994.

- *52 Dates for You and Your Mate*—52 tested dates for those who want to make their marriage come alive with fun, laughter, and good times together. Nashville: Thomas Nelson Publishers, 1993.

- *The Marriage Track*—How to keep your relationship headed in the right direction. Nashville: Thomas Nelson Publishers, 1992.

- *The Marriage Track Leader's Guide*—For leading Marriage Track Supper Clubs. Four couples get together four times for fun, fellowship and Bible Study. Available through Marriage Alive. To schedule a workshop with the Arps for your church, write to:

Entertaining Self